fiberarts
design
book
se7en

fiberarts design book

7

edited by
Susan Mowery Kieffer

LARK BOOKS

A Division of Sterling Publishing Co., Inc.
New York

Editor: Susan Mowery Kieffer
Art Director: Tom Metcalf
Assistant Art Director: Shannon Yokeley
Cover Designer: Barbara Zaretsky
Production Assistance: Laura Gabris
Editorial Assistance: Delores Gosnell
Interns: Katie Herzog, Carleigh Knight, Emma Marschall, Shelby Thompson
Valuable Assistance: Kathleen Holmes, Rosemary Kast, Deborah Morgenthal, Nancy Orban,
Sunita Patterson, Rob Pulleyn, Suzanne Tourtillott

Cover: **Morgan Clifford**. *Sources (detail)*, p. 142.
 Lampas woven, brocaded, painted warp; silk, linen; 30 by 64 in. Photo: Peter Lee

Front Flap: **Koos Van Den Akker**. *Circles Swing Coat*, p. 156.
Page 2: **Lauren Camp**. *Center Stage (detail)*, p. 13.
Back Flap: **Jorie Johnson**. *Pomegranate and Green Plum*, p. 168.
Back Cover: (top) **Liz Alpert Fay**. *Wheels of Fortune (detail)*, p. 152.
 (bottom) **Catherine L. Siterlet**. *Cedar Towers*, p. 65.

Library of Congress Cataloging-in-Publication Data

Fiberarts design book 7 / edited by Susan Mowery Kieffer.--1st ed.
 p. cm.
ISBN 1-57990-521-8 (hardcover)
 1. Textile crafts. 2. Fiberwork. I. Kieffer, Susan Mowery.

TT699.F522 2004
746--dc22

2003021636

10 9 8 7 6 5 4 3 2 1

First Edition

Published by Lark Books, a division of
Sterling Publishing Co., Inc.
387 Park Avenue South, New York, N.Y. 10016

© 2004, Lark Books

Distributed in Canada by Sterling Publishing,
c/o Canadian Manda Group, One Atlantic Ave., Suite 105
Toronto, Ontario, Canada M6K 3E7

Distributed in the U.K. by Guild of Master Craftsman Publications Ltd.
Castle Place, 166 High Street, Lewes, East Sussex, England BN7 1XU
Tel: (+ 44) 1273 477374, Fax: (+ 44) 1273 478606
Email: pubs@thegmcgroup.com, Web: www.gmcpublications.com

Distributed in Australia by Capricorn Link (Australia) Pty Ltd.
P.O. Box 704, Windsor, NSW 2756 Australia

If you have questions or comments about this book, please contact:
Lark Books
67 Broadway
Asheville, NC 28801
(828) 253-0467

Manufactured in China

ISBN 1-57990-521-8

contents

The *Fiberarts Design Book* series is a continuing celebration of the diversity and excellence found in this field we call the fiber arts, a field in which new ways of working with fiber are rapidly expanding our traditional definitions.

There is excitement in the air as new materials such as rubber, plastic, and metal are introduced and stand alongside the familiar fabric, thread, dye, and reed, and as experiments using processes such as photography and computer graphics weave their place into works alongside more traditional techniques such as stitching and dyeing.

Perhaps most exciting is the increasing acceptance of the fiber arts by major museums and galleries. Both are curating more fiber shows than ever before, and some galleries now devote their entire spaces to textile works. In addition, collectors are noticing the artistic vision and aesthetic sophistication of fiber artists and are showing their appreciation by adding fiber sculptures, wall hangings, and baskets to their collections.

This volume, number seven in the series, is our *FIBERARTS* Magazine juried compilation of works that have been completed since July 1998. The magazine has been promoting contemporary fiber art and offering a forum for the textile-arts community since 1976. The competition was, as it has been in the past, open to both professional and amateur artists working in a variety of techniques. We felt a rush of anticipation once again as the entries began filling boxes and then every available bit of wall space in the *FIBERARTS* office. There was a flurry of activity as nearly 6,000 entries from more than 30 countries were logged into a database.

Then began the jurying process—a pleasurable task, but no less daunting than for the other six *Design Books.* We used the same criteria we have in the past for deciding which pieces were juried in—aesthetic quality, technical expertise, and innovation—but it is never an easy matter to judge the work of an artist based solely on a slide or a transparency. We wanted to talk with the artists, ask them questions about their work and how they fabricated it, and to touch the pieces we were voting on. For, after all, this tactile nature of fiber is what attracts most artists to this medium. Who amongst us can resist handling fabric on the bolt in a store, and how much effort is needed to resist touching fiber works hanging on a gallery wall.

Judging has always been anonymous, but we couldn't help but recognize the works produced by well-known fiber artists as well as by artists covered in recent *FIBERARTS* articles. Many entries were submitted by artists new to us, however, and from their comments, we learned that they form an eclectic group—teachers, students, emerging artists, unrecognized artists who have been producing work for decades; others who dip in and out of the fiber scene, often committing to other mediums such as ceramics, wood, and metalwork; and still others who call themselves novices, nonprofessionals, or dabblers in the fiber arts.

The creations of the young artists resonate with enthusiasm and energy, and it is interesting to note how comfortable so many of them feel using plastics. As one young artist told us, "I was born in the seventies, so it feels natural to me to use plastic." A comment like this would have been quite unusual when the first *Design Book* was published in 1980. And it's both educational and fascinating to witness the stretching of the fiber vocabulary into unexpected directions. In all, there is an evident love of process in the dialog between the artists and the materials they choose and manipulate.

In previous *Design Books,* we noted the increasing number of artists who experimented with multidisciplinary surface-design approaches. In this current collection, we see a layering and rich complexity only hinted at 20 years ago. It's tempting to single out a few giants who have played such a fugue-like role in this development, but suffice it to say that today a single work can be dyed, painted, pieced, rusted, fused, couched, appliquéd, stitched, burned, and then encrusted with beads, metallic powders, and found objects. In addition, fiber artists are freely borrowing materials and embracing processes from other visual arts such as ceramics and sculpture. We think this predominance of interactive techniques has helped galleries, museums, and collectors to view textile works as artistic ends in themselves rather than as strictly utilitarian pieces.

One of the highlights in the production of a compendium of fiber works is noting the recurring themes that appeal to artists. There are pieces here that chronicle the cycles of life and death and works that are deeply concerned with nature and environmental issues. There are visual metaphors and textural narratives on society and its morals such as the excesses of consumerism and overcrowding. And sometimes these themes are dealt with in the diversionary form of puns or visual jokes that playfully nudge at our foibles and hypocrisies or jolt us into a deeper scrutiny of our beliefs. There are themes of immigration, emigration, family history, and love of home.

These various themes are here expressed in the vibrant work of a new generation of artists and in the mature work of artists who, through a clarity of vision and years of commitment, have developed signature styles. Welcome to *FIBERARTS Design Book 7.* We invite you to sit back and enjoy.

—The *FIBERARTS* Staff

quilts

3

Jen Swearington
UNITED STATES

Good Humor

Pieced, appliquéd, drawn, painted,
hand and machine embroidered,
free-motion machine quilted;
sheets, household fabric, gesso,
shellac, grease pencil, ribbon,
thread, monofilament; 34 by 24 in.

4

Judith Plotner
UNITED STATES

Caution

Machine pieced and appliquéd,
photo transfer, hand quilted,
machine embroidered; cotton;
26 by 18 in.

5

Bettina Andersen
DENMARK

Womanlife

Appliquéd, hand embroidered and
quilted; silk, cotton, synthetic fabric,
thread; 34 by 22 in.
Photo: Dennis Rosenfeldt

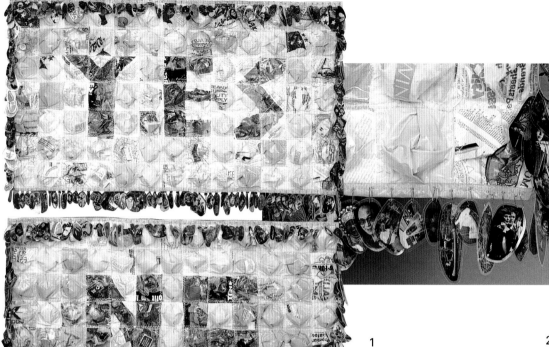

1

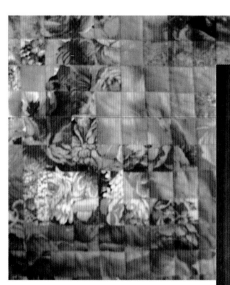

1

Pat Owoc
<small>United States</small>

Yes/No

Machine pieced and quilted, dyed;
plastic bags and wrappers, paper,
photographs, fabric, earring wires,
adhesive, batting, backing; 52 by 40
in. Photo: John Phelan

2

Lorraine Carthew
<small>Australia</small>

An Australian Bush Icon

Paper pieced; cotton; 65 by 83½ in.

*To push the boundaries of color
wash, I have turned to portrait
quilts. From a distance, the portrait
resembles a painting, but up close
it holds many surprises in the
fabrics chosen.*

2

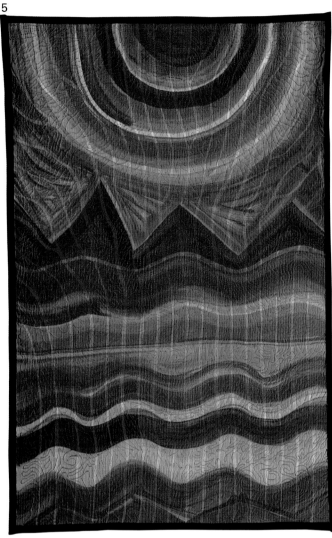

3

Donna Radner
UNITED STATES

Floating World #1

Machine pieced and quilted, fused; cotton batik, variegated thread; 64 by 56 in. Photo: Mark Gulezian

4

Jenny Hearn
SOUTH AFRICA

Fissures, Fossils, and Fragments 4: Red Thread

Machine and hand embroidered, machine pieced and quilted, appliquéd; cotton, embroidery thread, wool, curtaining; 60 by 60 in. Photo: Dion Cuyler

5

Phyllis Harper Loney
UNITED STATES

Landscape on a Young Planet

Dye painted, machine quilted; fiber-reactive dye, sodium alginate, silk habotai, silk noil, batting; 39 by 26 in. Photo: Denis Griggs

The layered patterns speak to me of the turbulent beauty of the millions of years of the creation of this world.

1

Barbara D. Cohen
UNITED STATES

Cityscape

Dyed, discharged, machine pieced, appliquéd, embroidered, quilted; cotton, cotton velveteen, cotton and rayon thread; 54 by 26 in.
Photo: Marcia Ward

2

Jeanne Williamson
UNITED STATES

Orange Construction Fence #6

Monoprinted, hand stamped, machine appliquéd and quilted; cotton, fabric paint, thread, batting; 40 by 30½ in. Photo: David Caras

4

5

3

Robin Schwalb
UNITED STATES

Strong Words

Stenciled, pieced, appliquéd, quilted; cotton; 36 by 36 in. Photo: Karen Bell

4

Lauren Camp
UNITED STATES

Center Stage

Machine appliquéd and quilted; silk, cotton, velvet, polyester, and mixed fabric, nylon and metallic thread, glass beads, batting; 37 by 23 in. Photo: Hawthorne Studio

5

Eliza Brewster
UNITED STATES

Too Many Targets
Too Little Time,

Hand appliquéd and quilted, discharged, photo transfer; cotton, ink, markers; 40 by 33 in. Photo: Sam Brewster

1

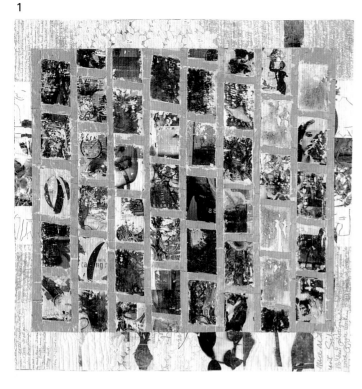

1

Joan Schulze
UNITED STATES

Beijing: The Summer Palace

Photocopied and glue-trans-
ferred images, pieced, machine
quilted; silk, cotton, paper,
metal leaf; 47 by 47 in.
Photo: Sharon Risedorph

2

Esterita Austin
UNITED STATES

Not Written in Stone

Fused, appliquéd, machine stitched,
painted; cotton, acrylic paint, polyester batting, rayon thread; 57 by 43
in. Photo: James Dee

*In my exploration of the quilt-making
process, I try to discover and reveal
a certain magical reality. I hope to
capture the feeling of wonder in the
surface design. To wonder where the
passage leads. To wonder from
where the light emanates. To wonder
what lies beyond the quilt surface.*

3

Rosemary Hoffenberg
UNITED STATES

Character Study

Hand dyed, shibori, block and screen
printed, painted, machine quilted;
cotton, canvas, ribbon; 74½ by 47 in.
Photo: David Caras

4

Marta Amundson
UNITED STATES

Swedish Design Sampler #3

Computer-altered photography,
machine embroidered, pieced, quilted; polymer clay, rayon thread,
hand-dyed and commercial cotton,
ink, handmade buttons; 86 by 48 in.
Photo: Gavin Ashworth

*Chairs are the essence of art and his-
tory in every culture. They come
from somewhere, and they are hon-
est in telling you their origins. Look
closely, and you will know that these
humble chairs are markers for
Stockholm, the city in my dreams.*

3

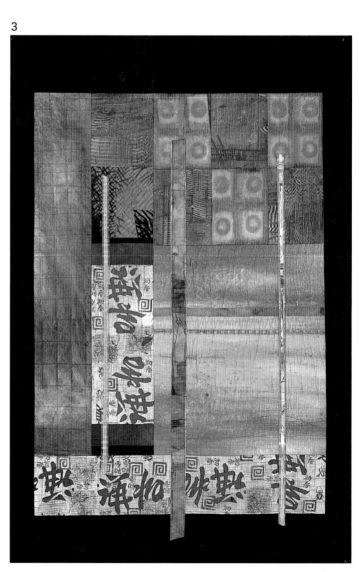

2

4

6

5

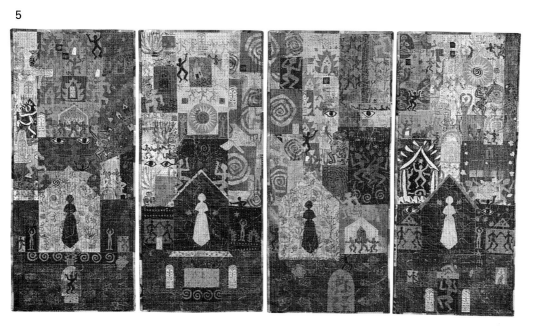

5
Natasha Kempers-Cullen
UNITED STATES

Hopes and Fears

Dyed, painted, block printed, collaged, machine stitched and quilted, beaded; fiber-reactive dye, textile paint, cotton, linen, silk, metallic and rayon thread, tulle, glass beads; each of four panels 47 by 21½ in. Photo: Dennis Griggs

6
Vickie Hallmark
UNITED STATES

Soul Searching

Collaged, machine quilted and embroidered, hand embroidered, beaded; hand dyed cotton and silk, thread, beads, foil, glass cabochons; 40 by 31 in.

All my work reflects my current life situation at the time of construction. This piece was made during a difficult time.

1

Janet Kurjan
UNITED STATES

Desert I

Machine pieced, free-motion machine quilted; hand-dyed cotton fabric, cotton thread, batting; 45 by 49 in. Photo: Jeff Clarke

2

Joanie SanChirico
UNITED STATES

Catacombs VI: Rust

Machine embroidered and quilted, appliquéd; hand-dyed cotton by various artists; 36 by 28 in.

I have an insatiable curiosity and love for ancient places and objects, devouring information and images of ancient civilizations. The result is art that is archeological in nature, mysterious in design, and reverent in interpretation.

1

2

3

Ree Nancarrow
UNITED STATES

Cut Bank

Screen printed, machine pieced and quilted; dye-stenciled and painted fabric, commercial fabric; 38½ by 42 in.

4

Carol Krueger
UNITED STATES

Kabuki, It's What's for Dinner

Machine pieced, machine and hand appliquéd, computerized machine-embroidered, hand quilted; rayon and polyester thread, cotton, batting, backing; 42 by 54 in.

A Star Trek fan takes his girl out for an evening of sushi overlooking the bright lights of Tokyo and the beautiful Mt. Fuji.

3

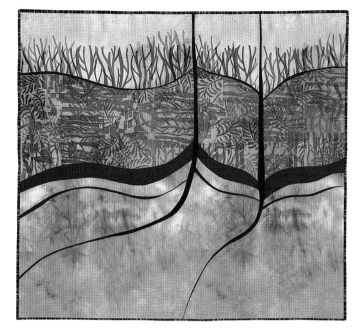

5

4

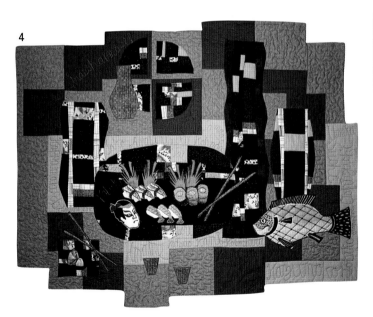

6

5

Frieda Anderson
UNITED STATES

Walks in the Woods

Machine pieced, quilted; hand-dyed cotton and thread, batting; 56½ by 65 in.

Everyday I walk in the woods with my dog George. The woods are tranquil like a church, and this piece reminds me of stained glass.

6

Randy Frost
UNITED STATES

Separation

Machine appliquéd and quilted, corded, embellished; commercial and hand-dyed cotton, yarn, perle cotton, beads, buttons, batting; 36 by 36 in. Photo: Joe Giunta

This is part of my zipper series—zippers as metaphors for things that happen in life in spite of the best-laid plans. This one opened at the bottom, leading to revelations of what might be concealed by the garment. What are we concealing beneath our outer garments?

1

Barbara Oliver Hartman
UNITED STATES

Celebration in Red

Machine appliquéd and quilted; hand-dyed and batik cotton; 84 by 84 in.

2

Michele Hardy
UNITED STATES

Tracking Center

Collaged, machine embroidered and quilted; cotton fabric, rayon, cotton, and metallic threads; 42½ by 49 in.

This piece was begun shortly after my family was forced to evacuate as a precaution for Hurricane Georges. Days of monitoring weather-tracking maps and continuous weather-news coverage were the inspiration for these images.

3

Liz Axford
UNITED STATES

Bamboo Boogie Woogie 2

Machine pieced and quilted, dyed; cotton broadcloth; 43 by 60 in. Photo: Hester & Hardaway

For years, my husband tried to convince me, unsuccessfully, to plant bamboo as a screen in front of our house. He finally wore me down. Though the bamboo has failed to take over the yard as I'd feared, it has instead taken over my psyche. I love everything about it: its grace and elegance, the way the light filters through it, the sound of it rustling in the breeze.

4

Charlotte Yde
DENMARK

Japanese Garden

Machine pieced and quilted, monoprinted, satin-stitch quilted; cotton, silk, old Japanese silk; 43⅓ by 48 in. Photo: Dennis Rosenfeldt

5

Leesa Zarinelli Gawlik
UNITED STATES

Land Marks

Hand dyed, machine pieced and quilted; silk, hemp, recycled-kimono silk-habotai lining, Laotian silk, batting, silk backing; 52¼ by 52¾ in. Photo: Petronella Ytsma

Each summer, I return to the US from Japan to visit family. During the flights, I am always fascinated by the graphic markings in the land, miles below. This piece reflects the passage into the midwest and my final destination.

3

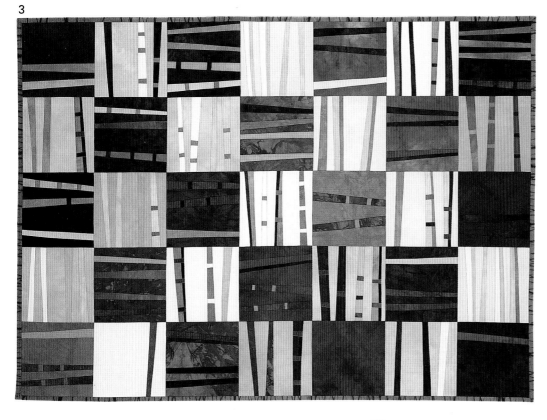

5

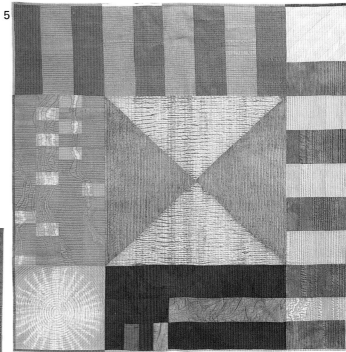

4

1

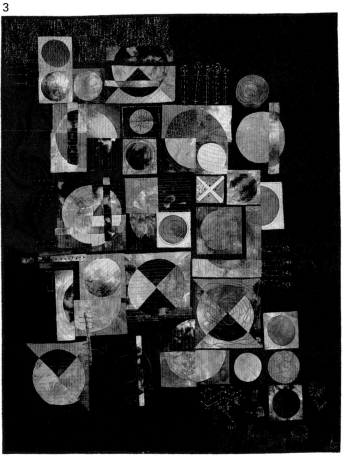

1

Eleanor McCain
UNITED STATES

Crab

Machine pieced and quilted; hand-dyed cotton; cotton backing, batting, thread; 90 by 90 in. Photo: Luke Jordon

This piece is an exploration of the colors found on the shell of the female Florida blue crab, Callinectes sapidus.

2

Lauren Rosenblum
UNITED STATES

Woman Fragmented

Screen printed, hand painted, discharged, hand quilted; cotton, fiber-reactive dyes, discharge paste, thread; 67 by 73 in. Photo: James Dee

3

Catherine Kleeman
UNITED STATES

Wheatfields

Collaged, machine quilted and embroidered, hand embroidered; commercial and hand-dyed cotton, netting; 37½ by 30 in.

Inspired by the irrigation patterns of the arid plains.

2

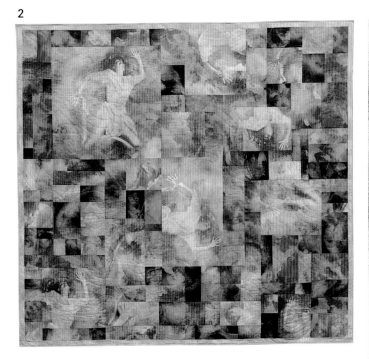

3

4

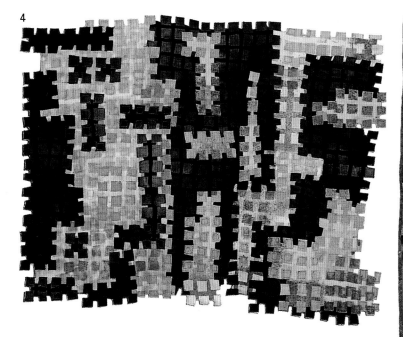

5

6

4

Judy Langille
UNITED STATES

Puzzle Grid

Collaged, printed, discharged, fused, machine quilted; cotton, dye, discharge paste; 34½ by 53 in.
Photo: Nancy Hlavacek

5

Sabina Palley
ENGLAND

Doris at a Quilt Show

Collaged, appliquéd, machine quilted, photographic transfer; cotton, thread, wadding; 66 by 45 in.
Photo: Stella Scordellis

I love trying to represent the human figure in paint or stitch. Whilst enjoying exhibitions, I am often intrigued by the visitors and the emotions they express.

6

Valerie S. Goodwin
UNITED STATES

Riverside Settlement

Pieced, appliquéd, fused, machine quilted; cotton, sheer fabric; 49 by 35 in. Photo: Richard Brunck

As an architect, I feel inspired by the idea of finding common ground between architectural language and the visual nature of quilting.

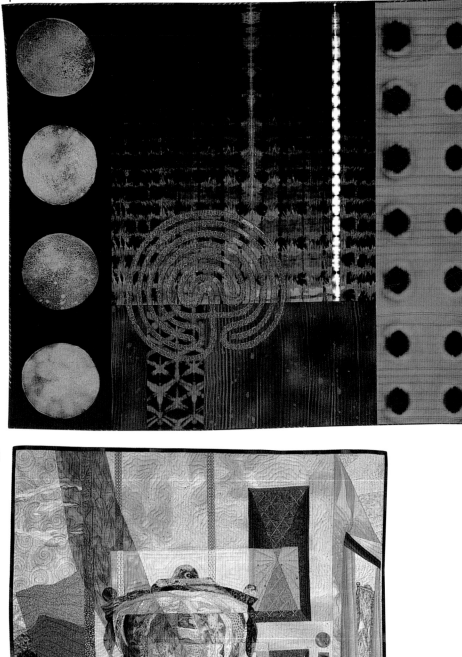

1
Linda Colsh
BELGIUM

Mole & Henge

Discharged, overdyed, machine pieced, appliquéd, machine quilted; metal, silk organza, cotton; 56 by 64 in.
Photo: Pol Leemans

Four times in two years I witnessed a mysterious and mystical henge phenomenon in Seoul—a mysterious shaft of luminous, bright light in the sky. The sight gave me understanding and a connection with ancient henge builders. The city of Seoul also has beneath it a vast and fascinating doppelganger city. With no maps, negotiating this underground warren requires learning the navigational skills of a mole.

2
Doria A. Goocher
UNITED STATES

Time's Release

Machine pieced and quilted, color washed; cotton, lamé; 42½ by 32½ in.
Photo: Michael Campos

3
Janet Steadman
UNITED STATES

Return to Go

Machine pieced and quilted; hand-dyed cotton; 50 by 36 in. Photo: Roger Schreiber

Sometimes we embark on new paths and meet new challenges; sometimes we take detours that prove to be beneficial, and sometimes the routes we choose turn out to be dead ends. Sometimes, it is just time to return to where we came from and to start over again.

4
Cher Cartwright
CANADA

In the Pink

Machine pieced and quilted; cotton fabric, dye; 36 by 52 in. Photo: Ken Mayer

5
Margit Morawietz
UNITED STATES

Gypsy II

Woven, machine appliquéd and quilted; cotton, silk, mixed fibers, rayon thread, shisha mirrors; 62 by 46 in.
Photo: Bob Springgate

3

5

4

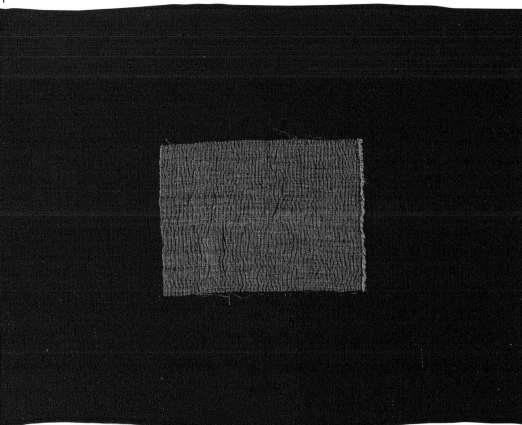

1

Judy McDermott
AUSTRALIA

Red Square

Hand stitched; hand-dyed thread; silk noil, silk obi, wool batting, linen binding, dye; 30 by 40 in. Photo: Andy Payne

2

Wendy Slotboom
UNITED STATES

Shades of Gray

Machine pieced and quilted; cotton; 71 by 58 in. Photo: Mark Frey

I live in Seattle where, in fall and winter, you either learn to love shades of gray, or you go a little nuts. I was fascinated by the subtle shades in the main print and enjoyed pairing it with the hot orange, a reminder that summer will arrive sooner or later.

3

Malka Dubrawsky
UNITED STATES

Chaim's Tree

Machine pieced and quilted, dyed, discharged; cotton; 32 by 26 in. Photo: Patrick Wong

This piece is particularly dear to me because it has two associations. In Hebrew, the word "Chaim" means life. In Jewish liturgy, the Torah is referred to as the "tree of life" to those who hold it fast. Chaim was also my grandfather's name, and this piece is dedicated to him.

4

Susan Webb Lee
UNITED STATES

O Hushed October Morning Mild

Machine pieced, edged, machine and hand quilted; hand-dyed cotton; 42 by 38½ in.

5

Odette Tolksdorf
SOUTH AFRICA

Broken Bones and Ladders

Machine pieced, hand quilted (by Inge Lailvaux); hand-dyed cotton, commercial cotton; 31 by 31 in.

3

5

4

1

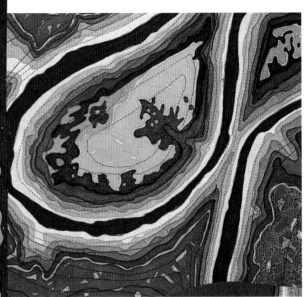

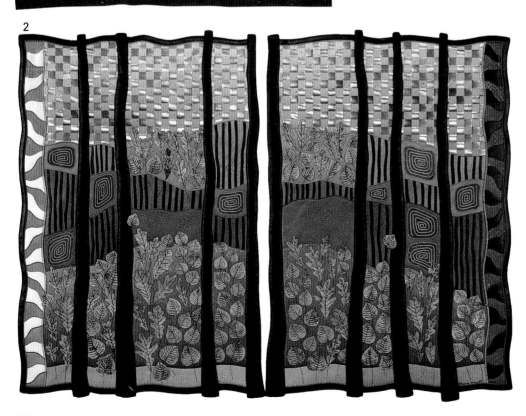

1

Donna June Katz
United States

Current

Hand painted, machine pieced and quilted; acrylic paint, unbleached muslin, batting; 50 by 29 in.
Photo: Tom Van Eynde

This piece was inspired by a raft trip in Utah and a hiking trip in the Grand Canyon.

2

Bernie Rowell
United States

Mountain Diptych: Golden Oaks

Hand painted, machine embroidered, collaged, appliquéd, pieced, quilted, embellished; paint, canvas, metallic fabric, metallic thread, beads; 48 by 60 in.
Photo: Tim Barnwell

3

Linda Gass
United States

Repairing the Night Sky

Hand painted, fused, machine quilted, trapunto, stitched; silk charmeuse, chiffon, organza, rhinestones, batting, rayon and metallic threads; 35 by 35 in.

This quilt is my wish to bring back the night sky—actually an easy problem to fix—we simply need to turn off the lights!

4

Astrid Hilger Bennett
United States

Three Conversations

Handpainted, monoprinted, machine quilted; cotton broadcloth, batting, dye; 44 by 75 in.

Although visually abstract, my work constantly mimics the daily life experiences of family, society, and the natural world, with a hefty dose of music to guide the hand.

3

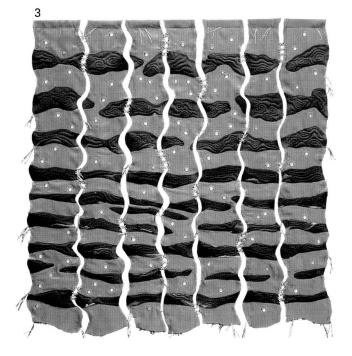

5

5

Marcia L. Whitney
United States

jihad

Machine quilted, fused, appliquéd,
beaded; cotton, decorative thread,
beads; 36 by 30 in. Photo: Jay York

4

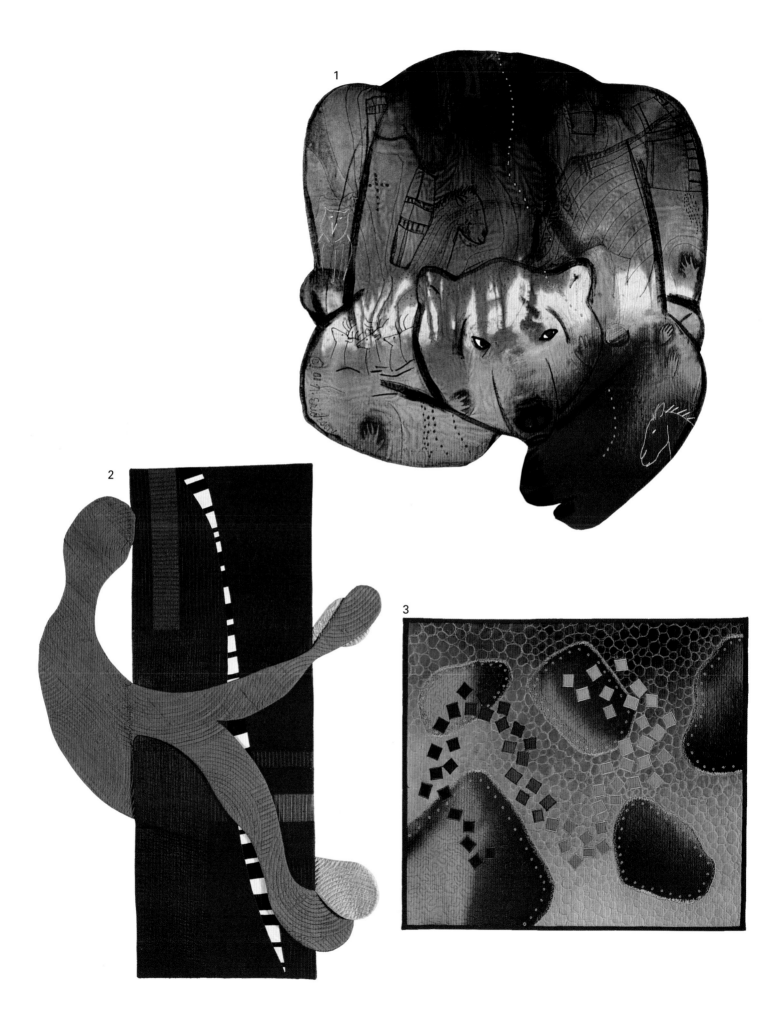

4

1
Nancy N. Erickson
UNITED STATES

Historian

Machine stitched, painted, appliquéd, quilted; velvet, satin, cotton, felt filler, fabric paint, charcoal, paintstick; 41 by 36½ in.

This polar bear has some of his history emblazoned on his body. I was trying out the brightest reds and blues I could make on the velvet.

2
Jane Einhorn
UNITED STATES

Hugging the Straight and Narrow

Machine pieced, quilted, hand sewn; silk, cotton batik, batting; 43 by 31 in. Photo: James Hart

I'm an artist and a psychotherapist. Many of my images are inspired by pondering on how we go about being human.

3
Liz Berg
UNITED STATES

Sea Star Study #4

Raw-edge appliquéd, fused, machine quilted and embroidered; cotton (dyed by Caryl Bryer Fallert), rayon thread; 19¼ by 22¾ in. Photo: Jim Ferreira

This is the fourth in a series based on a closeup of the underside of a starfish. I use nature as an inspiration for abstract work which explores color and movement.

4
Barbara Mullan
AUSTRALIA

Quadtulip

Quilted, reverse appliquéd, strip pieced, machine embroidered; silk, cotton; 59 by 39 ½ in.
Photo: Michael Mullan

5
Jane A. Sassaman
UNITED STATES

Ground Cover I

Machine quilted and appliquéd; cotton; 28 by 57 in.
Photo: Brian Blauser

A slice of life from the forest floor.

5

1

3

4

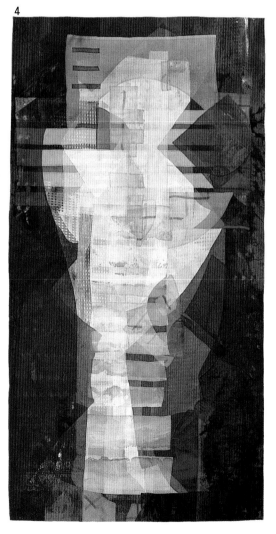

2

1

Joan M. Ladendorf
UNITED STATES

Quartet

Machine quilted, couched, fused; cotton, handwoven fabric, felt, yarn, thread, cotton batting; 75½ by 47½ in.

2

Cherilyn Martin
NETHERLANDS

Fresco I

Machine quilted and stitched, painted; batik and commercial silk; 50 by 35 in.

Design developed from a study of Roman architecture, influenced by fragments and surfaces of architectural ruins and wall frescoes.

3

Lisa S. Binkley
UNITED STATES

Recapitulata (Echo Flower)

Machine appliquéd and quilted, hand embroidered, quilted, and beaded; cotton, polyester, and rayon thread, embroidery cotton, glass and crystal beads; 23 by 23 in.
Photo: Mario Quintana

I enjoy creating my own hybrid flowers in quilt form and then giving them official plant names.
Recapitulata *seemed an appropriate species name for a flower whose form is a repeat or echo of the form in its very center.*

4

Emily Richardson
UNITED STATES

Elder Fire and Shadow

Hand stitched, appliquéd, and quilted; acrylic paint, silk, cotton; 61½ by 32 in. Photo: Rick Fine

5

Judy B. Dales
UNITED STATES

Fantasy Form #6117: Not a Calico Chicken

Machine pieced, appliquéd, and quilted; cotton, marbled fabric, tulle, chiffon, cotton batting and backing; 47 by 61 in. Photo: Mike McCormick

This is part of my Fantasy Form series—designs derived from doodles. Many of the fabrics were marbled by Marjorie Lee Bevis. The main portion of the quilt was pieced, but transparent fabrics were layered in the background areas to enhance the design and add a watercolor effect.

6

Ann Harwell
UNITED STATES

Church in the Wildwood

Machine pieced, free-hand machine quilted; hand-dyed and commercial cotton; 71 by 65 in. Photo: Lynn Ruck

1

Jackie Evans
UNITED STATES

On the Way to the Bakery

Appliquéd, embroidered, machine quilted; hand-dyed and commercial fabrics; 80 by 51 in.

2

Marcia Stein
UNITED STATES

Sidewalk Cafe

Machine appliquéd, pieced, and quilted, fused; cotton, lamé; 43 by 67 in.

2

3

3
Dominie Nash
UNITED STATES

Stills from a Life 4

Machine appliquéd and quilted, drawn, other surface-design techniques; cotton, silk; 60 by 60½ in.

It's surprising to look at familiar objects in a new context, such as when setting up a still-life composition. Often the homeliest or most ordinary things have the most interesting shapes and patterns when abstracted and made to interact with each other. The challenge of exploring and developing these relationships into a satisfying arrangement and then translating it into fabric on a two-dimensional plane keeps me interested in pursuing this series.

4
Elizabeth Brimelow
ENGLAND

Appeltrebankes

Double-sided quilted, hand and machine stitched, appliquéd, reverse appliquéd, slashed, tied; seven layers of silk; 84 by 84 in. Photo: Peter Jenion

Appeltrebankes is the name of an ancient field near my home. Landscape is my inspiration. It is where I live, what I look at, what I draw, and what I stitch.

4

1

2

3

Ricki Moffat
CANADA

Elijah's Cups

Hand pieced, appliquéd, and quilted, beaded, embroidered; cotton, silk, floss, beads, costume jewelry, found objects, buttons, charms; 36 by 27 in. Photo: Geo Photographics

4

Sandra Hoefner
UNITED STATES

The Day He Left for America

Hand appliquéd and quilted, embellished; commercial cotton, some overdyed, piping; 77 by 72 in. Photo: Brian Allen

My inspiration was a photo taken of my father and two of his brothers on the day he got on a boat from Sweden to America. My works are narrative, with humorous overtones.

1

Susie Krage
UNITED STATES

Beside Herself: Jennifer

Computer-manipulated image, printed, machine pieced and quilted; cotton, inkjet, cotton batting; 24½ by 27½ in. Photo: Mark Gulezian

2

Sandi Cummings
UNITED STATES

Bicentennial

Screen printed, machine pieced, appliquéd, and quilted; hand-dyed cotton, commercial fabric, fabric paint; 52 by 72 in. Photo: Don Tuttle

4

5

5

Ursula Baumung
GERMANY

Silence

Machine sewn, reverse appliquéd, fused; net, newspaper, fabric scrap; 66½ by 46½ in.

6

Susan Mosler
UNITED STATES

Star Catchers

Hand quilted and embroidered, appliquéd, painted, beaded, printed; cotton, cotton blend, batting, gesso, watercolor pencil, glue, ink, glass beads; 56 by 37 in.

6

1

Caryl Bryer Fallert
United States

Spirogyra #1

Hand dyed and painted,
machine pieced, appliquéd,
quilted; cotton, fiber-reactive
dye, batting, thread; 65 by 44 in.

2

Clare Plug
New Zealand

Promenade

Machine pieced and quilted, discharged, dyed; cotton; 40 by 94 in.
Photo: Clive Ralph

*Tide marks left on the sand; grey-
wake stones blanketing the city
beach; formal gardens bordered
by narrow, shingle paths; rows of
Norfolk Island pines, their needles
patterning the pavement—an endless source for reflection.*

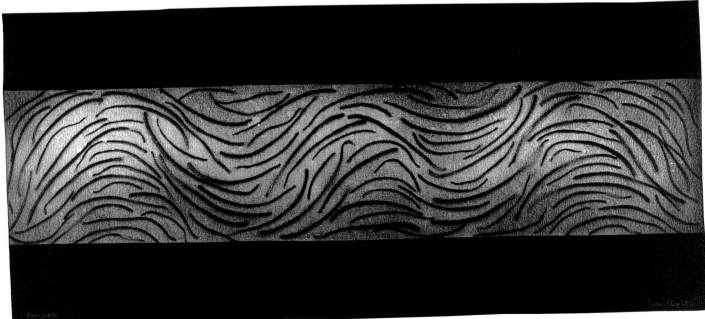

3

Jette Clover
UNITED STATES

Yellow Wall II

Dyed, collaged, hand printed and
quilted; cotton, silk. 53 by 35 in.

*I find a compelling beauty in the
various stages of decay and disin-
tegration and the haphazard layering and marks caused by time and
the elements. My direct inspiration
is the worn collages of image and
text on urban walls.*

4

Patricia Mink
UNITED STATES

Terra Incognita

Inkjet printed, machine embroidered
and quilted; satin acetate, brocade,
lace, gold lamé, thread, cotton batting; 40 by 60 in.

1

Clare Smith
NEW ZEALAND

'X' Marks the Spot

Raw-edge appliquéd, machine quilted; recycled clothing, perle cotton, batting; 60 by 55 in. Photo: Helen Mitchell

This quilt was made in response to a newspaper article which spoke of discrimination by employers and insurance companies against people with faulty DNA, "The Genetic Underclasses." The X marks the spot where the DNA is not perfect. The design is based on the "wagga" or utility quilt which was often made from discarding clothing.

2

Jane Burch Cochran
UNITED STATES

For Dilsey

Machine pieced, hand quilted, appliquéd, embellished; fabric, beads, buttons, paint, sequins, recycled apron, gloves, handkerchief; 63 by 61 in. Photo: Pam Monfort

The Rabbit Hash Book Club decided to tackle William Faulkner's The Sound and the Fury. This quilt is named for the character Dilsey, the black woman who was my favorite character.

3

Dina Baumane
LATVIA

Winter Garden

Appliquéd, dyed, painted, machine quilted; silk; 3⅓ by 3⅓ in.

Loneliness and estrangement, as a contemporary regularity of globalization, are shown in my piece. Here you see men and women as a symbolical tree with cut roots (no stability) and tops (destroyed, unhappy).

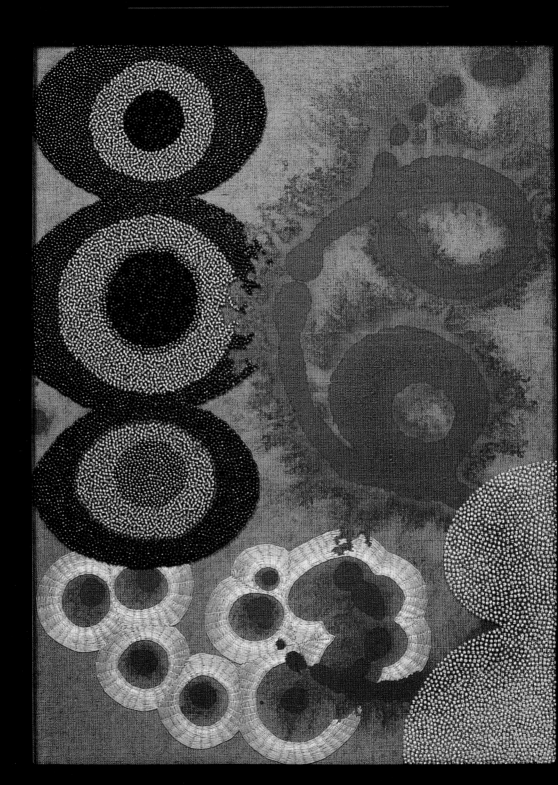

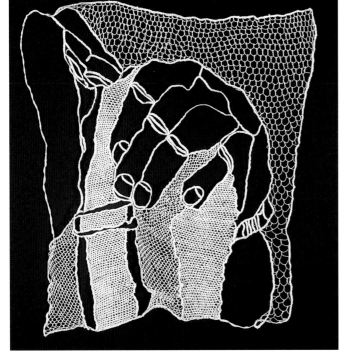

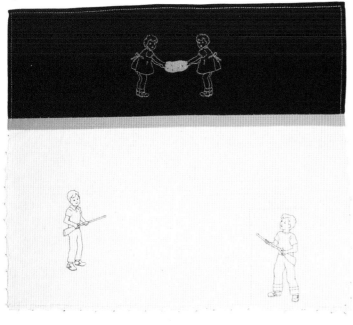

previous page

Karin Birch
UNITED STATES

Serpentine

Beaded, couched, painted; linen, embroidery floss, glass seed beads, acrylic paint; 22 by 18 in.

1

Maggy Rozycki Hiltner
UNITED STATES

The Monsanto Twins Try a Little Genetic Engineering

Appliquéd, stitched; cotton, felt; 13 by 16 in.

2

Dorie Millerson
CANADA

Hand with Buckle

Lace needleworked; backing cloth, cotton thread; 10 by 10 in.

This piece was inspired by a family photograph. The image depicts my late father's hand on my shoulder. It is stitched in a technique that involves creating a lace structure with a needle onto a temporary backing cloth and removing it when complete.

4

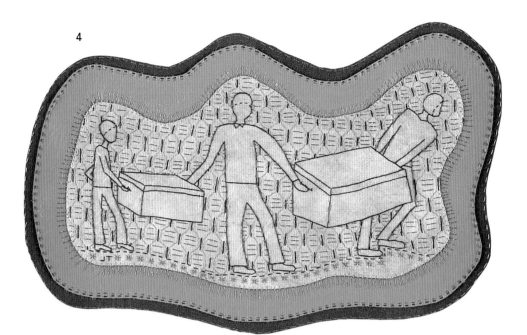

5

Linda H. Konya
UNITED STATES

John

Embroidered, appliquéd, wrapped; linen, wool, cotton floss; 15 by 17 in. Photo: Carla Steckley

6

Carol Ventura
UNITED STATES

The Rules

Tapestry crocheted; linen; 15 by 7 in. Photo: John S. Cummings

Tapestry crochet differs from ordinary crochet in its texture, tension, and how colors are manipulated. Two or more yarns are worked at the same time to create intricate or simple motifs. One yarn is carried while another is worked over it.

5

6

3

Tilleke Schwarz
NETHERLANDS

Rites

Hand embroidered, stitched; dyed linen, cotton and silk yarn, lace; 25½ by 25½ in. Photo: Rob Mostert

The title of this work refers to texts and images that are mostly part of incomprehensible contemporary rites of human society.

4

Tricia Lane
UNITED STATES

Three Young Men Carry Two Large Trunks

Embroidered, appliquéd, quilted; vinyl, cotton thread; 7½ by 12 in.

As a child of the seventies and eighties, I have very fond memories of living with plastic. It feels natural to combine synthetic fabrics with natural fabrics to document my life.

1

Margaret Cusack
UNITED STATES

Cause and Effect

Machine appliquéd; metallic fabric, buttons, thread, metal frame; 8 by 10 in. Photo: Alex Cao

2

Colleen O'Rourke
UNITED STATES

Lazy Eye

Embroidered; cotton, seed beads, thread; 15 by 19 in.

3

Carol Burns
UNITED STATES

Rainy Day on the Isle of Spice

Embroidered; fabric, embroidery floss; 16½ by 13¼ in.

4

Heidrun Schimmel
GERMANY

Hanging at the Wall I

Stitched; silk organza, thread; 46⅓ by 20 by 6 in.

For many years I've been stitching by hand exclusively because I am interested in the connection between thread and time, and thread and human.

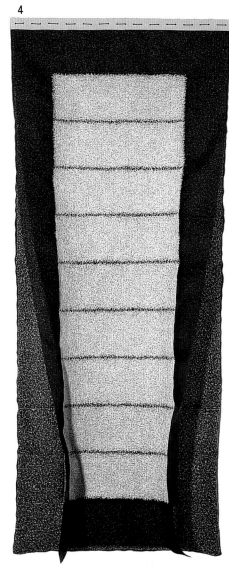

4

5

Kyoung Ae Cho
UNITED STATES

Scroll II

Constructed, hand stitched; silk
organza, balsam-fir needles, rayon
thread, wood. 9 by 142 in. Variable.

6

Jacy Diggins
UNITED STATES

Checked in Process

Pleated, stitched, pinned; vintage
silk, pins, thread; 31 by 16 in.
Photo: Andrew Neuhart

1

2

3

4

1

Tricia Coulson
<small>UNITED STATES</small>

Woman's Work

Hand stitched; vintage fabric, pearls, sequins, beads; 18 by 18 in. Photo: David Lee

2

Beth Barron
<small>UNITED STATES</small>

Repair II

Hand stitched; fabric, adhesive bandages, beads, thread, paint; 12 by 15½ in. Photo: P. Ytsma

How often have we applied a bandage when there was no external wound, just to relieve the wailing of a child? And I laughed at myself as I wished it were as simple to repair a broken heart.

3

Alison Withers
<small>AUSTRALIA</small>

Relic

Free-motion machine embroidered; cotton, polyester, thread, paint; 25 by 7 ½ in.

I love the old building materials that are used in rural Australia. They tell me a story of what life was like before I arrived.

4

Cindy Hickok
<small>UNITED STATES</small>

Blessed Excess

Free-motion stitched; rayon thread, colored pencils, shredded money; 22 by 14 in. Photo: Rick Wells

A look at the way we keep piling things on, always in excess—big cars, big TV, loud noise, phones for each hand, food, food, food.

5

Dianne Shullenberger
<small>UNITED STATES</small>

Bluejay Feather

Layered, collaged, machine stitched; silk, cotton, and nylon fabric, thread; 25 by 21 in. Photo: Lori Landau

5

1

3

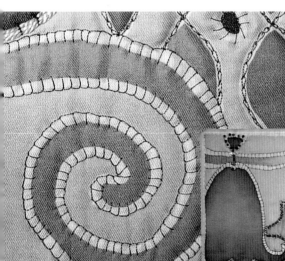

2

4

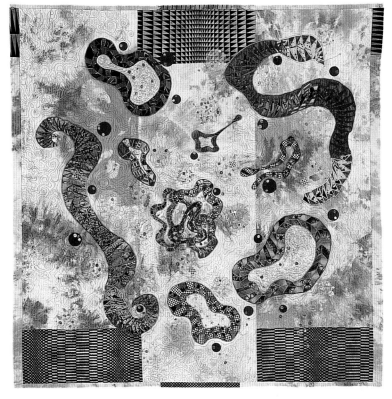

5

1

Gabriella Verstraeten
AUSTRALIA

Captured

Machine embroidered; silk, padding, nylon and rayon thread; 8 by 8 in.
Photo: Gene Verstraeten

2

Christine Ambrose
UNITED STATES

Bluebells

Dye painted, wax resist, beaded, quilted, embroidered; silk twill, beads, cotton, rayon, and silk thread, batting; 11⅜ by 19¼ in.
Photo: Carol Krueger

Beauty is all around us. Creativity lights up my life and inspires happiness and contentment in me.

3

Sally-Ann Boyd
ENGLAND

Fulfilling Expectations

Seminole and strip patchworked; hand-dyed silk, cotton; 108 by 72 in.
Photo: John Jameson

This is the sixth in my "Great Expectations" series.

4

Ethel Shulam
UNITED STATES

Ode to K. and K.

Dyed, overdyed, machine embroidered, appliquéd, pieced, and quilted, fused; cotton, sheer synthetic fabric, cotton, rayon, and metallic thread; 51 by 51 in.
Photo: David Caras

Two of my favorite artists are Kandinsky and Klee.

5

Mary Ruth Smith
UNITED STATES

Tribulation

Compacted, overlaid French knots; cotton, embroidery floss; 10 by 10 in.

1

Anna Torma
CANADA

Storybook Pages I

Hand embroidered and stitched; silk, patchwork base, silk thread; 40 by 40 in. Photo: Balint Zsako

2

Susan Boardman
UNITED STATES

Fireworks with Mother, 1879

Embroidered, dye painted, needlelace, appliquéd, quilted; cotton, fiber reactive dye, embroidery floss, beads, leather, wire; 6½ by 9¼ in. Photo: Jack Weinhold

My inspiration comes from women's journals and letters in the Nantucket Historical Association collection.

3

Myriam Tripet
SWITZERLAND

Sous-Bois

Machine stitched; wool, cotton, silk, metallic thread; 16 by 12 in.

4

Reina Mia Brill
UNITED STATES

Twirlupp

Knitted; copper wire, brass, wood; 18 by 8 by 5 in.

The knitted-wire material is very malleable and can be manipulated into a wide variety of shapes to achieve movement, surprise, and a sense of animation—all characteristics that I try to incorporate into each piece.

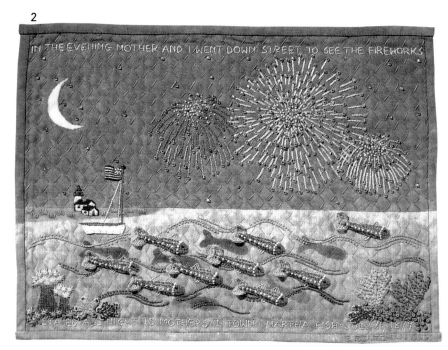

4

5

Marta Herbertson
Australia

Many Paths

Stitched, padded; raffia; 12¼ by 12½ in. diameter. Photo: Lloyd Hissey

6

Jeanette Carr
United States

Thread Castle

Machine stitched in hoop; water-soluble stabilizer, thread; 15 by 3 by 1 in.

My intent was to suggest strength through fragility. The use of thread alone to construct a house presented many challenges and reinforced just how fragile our home, our happiness, and our lives truly are.

6

1

2

3

5

1

Beth Nobles
UNITED STATES

Selma Story: March for the Vote, 1965

Hand and machine embroidered, stitched, stretched; silk, cotton, painted silk, plexiglass, cotton and rayon thread; 6 by 29 by 18 in.
Photo: Mark Tade

Some of my recent work is about our history in the Civil Rights Movement. What I hope it does for the viewer is to question what we will do about the issues of today, including the issues of racism and acceptance.

2

Gillian Ann Elliott
ENGLAND

Night Life

Machine embroidered, pieced; cotton, silk, velvet, wool, felt, thread, paint, dye, ink, bleach; 42 by 29 in.

3

Alice Gant
UNITED STATES

Best Friends

Neo-reverse appliquéd, machine stitched; commercial fabric, thread; 36 by 36 in. Photo: Andrew Gillis

4

Jennifer Sargent
UNITED STATES

The Cold Season

Hand colored, distressed, perforated, paper crocheted; paper, wire; 20 by 32 in. Photo: Alan McCoy

This work relates to the garden—that marginal area between civilization and wilderness. It is a place that parallels my art making, where repetitive processes allow time to integrate thought, action, and materiality and where the act of layering allows one surface both to reveal and conceal another.

5

Robin L. Bergman
UNITED STATES

In the Beginning (Torah cover)

Machine knitted, hand finished, sewn; rayon chenille, silk, rayon viscose, metallic yarn; 19 by 13 by 6 ½ in. Photo: Gordon S. Bernstein

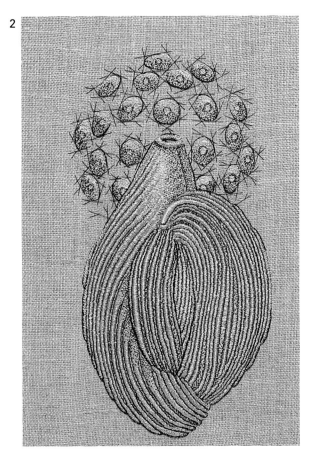

1

Nancy Geller
CANADA

Miriam's Well

Stitched; linen, embroidery floss, metallic thread; 4⅝ by 4 in.

This piece is a biography of Miriam, sister of Moses. To me, it is both a challenge and an inspiration to explore and interpret fragments of the Old Testament. I want my work to reflect the grace and the relevance of this great Book.

2

John Hawthorne
UNITED STATES

Aura 1, MF: Protozoa Foraminiferia with Radiolaria

Embroidered; linen, cotton floss, metallic thread; 6 by 4 in. Photo: Kathryn Wetzel

This work was inspired by my perception of how others perceive me.

3

Sumi Nakano
JAPAN

Koto

Hand sewn, appliqued, embroidered; kimono, thread; 3½ by 3½ ft.

4

Eleanor Hannan
CANADA

Found Objects from Dreams

Machine embroidered; linen, thread; 4 by 6 in. Photo: Ted Clarke

4

5

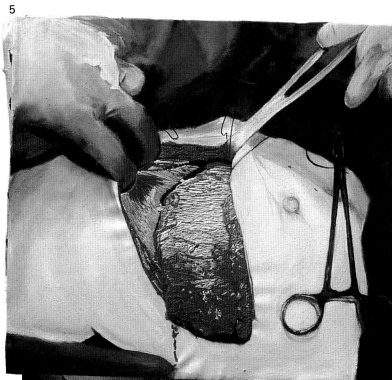

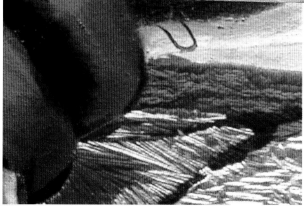

5

Bev McNaughton
CANADA

Reduction #2

Painted, embroidered; silk/cotton fabric, oil paint, silk and cotton embroidery thread; 12⅓ by 11¾ in.
Photo: John Tamblyn

In my most recent work, I create oil-painted reproductions of actual surgical operations. In this case, the operation was a breast reduction. Embroidery covers the portion of the painting where the raw flesh would have been exposed.

6

Peggy Moulton
UNITED STATES

Van Gogh's Cat

Embroidered; cotton, silk, polyester fabric, thread; 7 by 9 in.
Photo: Kirby Moulton

6

1

2

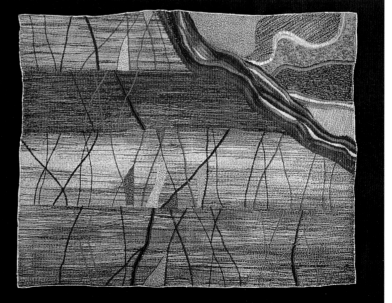

2

Stephen Beal
UNITED STATES

Last Light on I-25

Basketweave and continuous
stitched, overstitched, backstitched;
fabric, cotton floss; 11½ by 16½ in.
Photo: Joe Coca

3

Melinda Snyder
UNITED STATES

Landforms: Bay View

Machine stitched, painted; cloth, thread;
18 by 21 in. Photo: Geoffrey Carr

_From a distance my embroideries are
not immediately recognizable as being
made of cloth and thread. Upon closer
inspection, the density of the stitches
captures the eye and differentiates
them from a drawing or painting._

1

Carol Shinn
UNITED STATES

Winter Constellation

Computer-generated photography,
free-style machine stitched; broadcloth, canvas, paper-backed fusible
web, thread; 13¼ by 18¼ in.

_This piece records the mood of a
specific car, season, and landscape.
Like others in my old-car series, it
also speaks metaphorically about
human aging._

4

Bette Levy
<small>United States</small>

Into the Maelstrom

Hand embroidered; silk thread, wire; 20 by 15 by 2 in. Photo: Dawghans

This is based on a photograph I encouraged my husband to take. We were standing by a rapidly moving creek and noticed a tiny six-inch whirlpool in the shallows. I was fascinated by being able to see so many images simultaneously—the creek rock, the water, the ripples in the water, and the reflections of the surrounding woods and sky.

5

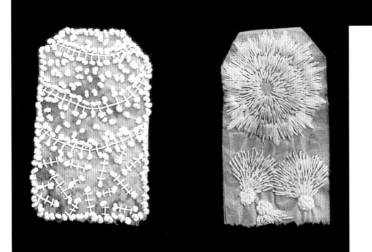

5

Miyuki Imai
<small>United States</small>

Landscape 5

Tea stained, hand stitched; tea bags, tea, thread; 22 by 18½ in.
Photo: Tom Mills

I draw landscapes of Penland by stitching, showing fireflies flying in the air, maple seeds falling down in May, moss wet with dew, or milkweed popping up from the seed pod.

1

2

3

4

5

1

Bonnie Ward Klehr
UNITED STATES

Eternal Motion

Hand embroidered; fabric, thread; 2½ by 3 in. Photo: Jim Prinz

2

Martha Bruin Degen
UNITED STATES

Changing Times

Painted, machine and hand quilted, appliquéd, embroidered; canvas, cotton, fiber paint, sequins, glass beads; 37 by 26 in. Photo: Gentry Photography

Adolescents today face different challenges growing up than baby boomers. I have chosen Girl Scout badges as a traditional American symbol to represent these differences. Did we, the baby boomers, create the new and more serious challenges?

3

Elly Smith
UNITED STATES

Gift Angel of Fashionable Death

Cross stitched, back stitched; cotton, metallic thread; 16 by 15 in.

4

Anne Honeyman
ENGLAND

Guilt

Machine and hand embroidered; cotton, rayon thread; 16 by 12 in.

5

Mary Frances Reymann
UNITED STATES

Envelope Squares in B and W

Machine stitched; fabric, thread; 17 by 17 by 1 in.

1

3

Lenda DuBose
UNITED STATES

Clouds

Embroidered, dyed, beaded; linen, tea, embroidery floss, thread, beads; 5¼ by 4½ in.

4

Suzanne Gregg
UNITED STATES

Cardinal Sin

Machine embroidered; canvas, rayon thread; 31 by 21 in.
Photo: Chris Stewart

How many children were sacrificed by the silence of the bishops and cardinals in an attempt to save the reputation of the Catholic Church?

1

Donald G. Talbot
UNITED STATES

Sometimes She Thought She Was Alone in the Universe

Deconstructed, reassembled; knitted sweaters, plywood; 24 by 41 by 9 in. Photo: Jay York

2

Linda Behar
UNITED STATES

Children of South Africa

Embroidered; cotton, paint, embroidery floss; 5 by 25 in.
Photo: Dean Powell.
Detail photo: David Caras

3

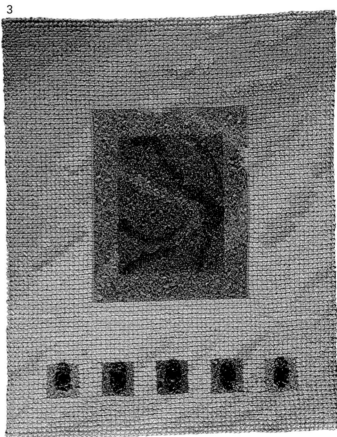

2

4

6

5

5

Caroline Dahl
UNITED STATES

An Excess to Remember

Embroidered, beaded; embroidery
floss, metallic braid, glass beads;
16½ by 16½ in. Photo: Colormetro

6

Riitta-Liisa Haavisto
FINLAND

Madam Blue

Hand embroidered; silk, cotton,
linen, viscose; 14¼ by 11¼ in.
Photo: Matti Huuhua

*Inspired by the stunning hats of the
Royal Ascot Race.*

1

Mary Bero
UNITED STATES

Sorceress

Embroidered; cotton, silk, rayon; 7½ by 6⅝ in. Photo: Jim Wildeman

2

Marta Ziemirska-Panek
CANADA

Medusa

Crocheted, embroidered, wrapped; cotton, silk, viscose, wool, nylon, metallic thread; 14 by 8 in. diameter Photo: Tracy Clare

The technique adapted from basketry influenced the design.

3

Pat Klein
UNITED STATES

The Stitcher

Embroidered; linen, cotton floss; 18 by 14 in.

I was going to title this piece "The Alchemist" for it represents the transformative (butterfly-head) power of the stitcher—to create beauty and comfort.

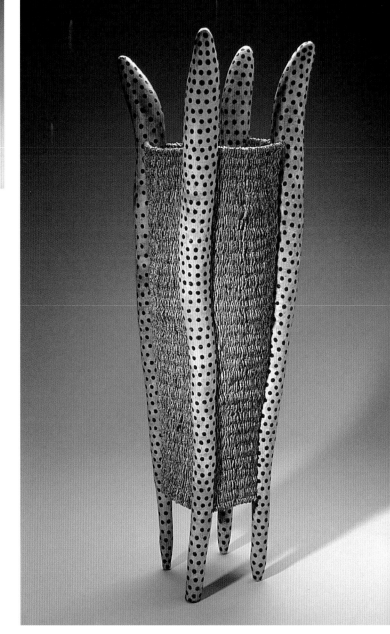

previous page

Dona Anderson
UNITED STATES

Silo

Wrapped, stitched; patterned paper, reed, cotton thread; 16 by 8 by 5 in.
Photo: Jerry McCollum

1

Stephen Kostyshyn
UNITED STATES

Twisty-Stick Vessel

Turned, woven, assembled; reed, palm, wood, red stick, willow, clay; 24 by 12 in.

Working with three materials—fiber, clay, and wood—has opened a world of design forms that I was previously unable to obtain with just one medium.

2

Don Weeke
UNITED STATES

Dot Column

Woven, burned; gourd, reed, palm-seed frond; 47¼ by 16½ by 16½ in.
Photo: Rodney Nakamoto

3

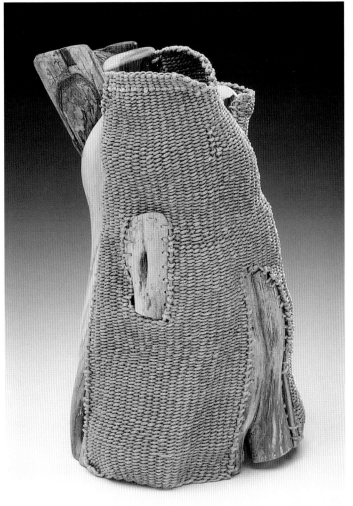

5

4

3

Jo Hoersten
UNITED STATES

Lilac + Linen II

Twined; lilac wood, waxed linen, linseed oil; 9 by 5 by 5 in.
Photo: Don Rutt

*When a very old lilac tree in our yard
blew down, I discovered the beauty
of the wood and knew I had to work
with it.*

4

Amy L. Kropitz
UNITED STATES

*How Fast Does your World Spin:
Neighboring Woodlands*

Woven, hand embroidered; hand-
dyed reed, hand-dyed silk, cotton;
19 by 9 in. Photo: Robert Ellis

5

Susan Stone
UNITED STATES

Temple Bells

Twined, wrapped; iris leaves, bones,
waxed linen, beads, bells, chamois
lining; 9½ by 8 by 1½ in.
Photo: Garth Dowling

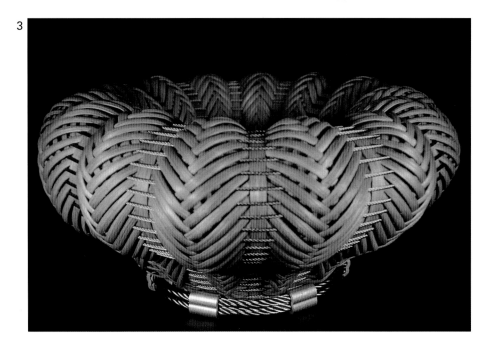

1

Virginia Kaiser
AUSTRALIA

Stiletto

Coiled, stitched; pine needles, jacaranda, cotton and linen thread; 13½ by 7½ by 16 in.
Photo: John Lascelles

Torturing our feet in the 60s in the name of beauty! Ouch!

2

Jeanne Drevas
UNITED STATES

Planet II

Constructed, glued, sewn; phragmites, white pine bark, red osier, waxed linen, interior form; 10½ by 24 in. diameter.

3

Carole Hetzel
UNITED STATES

Brendan #54

Hand-dyed, double-woven continuous construction; reed, black walnut dye, stainless steel cable; 11 by 24 by 24 in.

This work is about peace and harmony. Natural reed surrounds and supports the endless flow of stainless steel cable, and this balanced interaction between what would appear to be unrelated matter symbolizes how everything in life is perfectly interconnected.

4

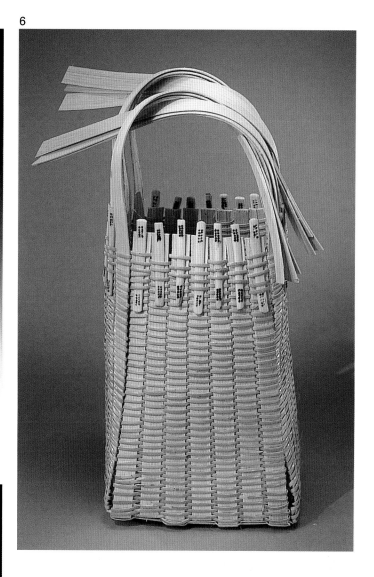

6

5

4

Catherine L. Siterlet
UNITED STATES

Cedar Towers

Plain woven; cedar bark, leather; 18 by 10 by 5 in.

The rough, stringy bark of cedar when peeled away, and split reveals an inner core of flexible and unlimited possibilities for shaping forms.

6

Norma Andersen Fox
UNITED STATES

Ten by Ten

Woven; reed, cane, Mah Jong bone counters; 14 by 6 by 6 in. Photo: Charles Kennard

5

Arlene K. McGonagle
UNITED STATES

Lines of Verse #2

Woven; wire, silk paper, handmade paper; 10 by 8½ in. Photo: James Beards

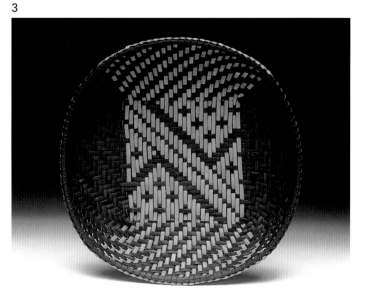

1

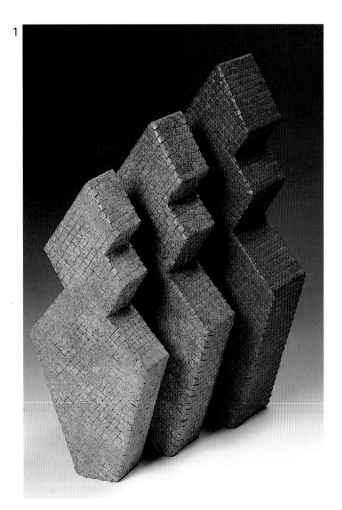

2

3

1

Jackie Abrams
UNITED STATES

The Guardians

Plaited; cotton paper, acrylic paint, medium. Photo: Jeff Baird

2

Billie Ruth Sudduth
UNITED STATES

Crimson Tide

Japanese twill-basketry construction, plaited, dyed; cut-reed splints, henna and madder dye; 13 by 15 by 15 in. Photo: Paul Jeremias

The feminine form evokes passion through movement and color. An object to hold not your objects but your interest.

3

Tressa Sularz
UNITED STATES

Journey

Twill-woven, dyed, lashed; Hamburg cane, rattan, waxed linen; 1½ by 8 in. diameter. Photo: Peter Lee

4

Kay Khan
UNITED STATES

Quest

Quilted, pieced, appliquéd, hand and machine stitched, constructed; silk, cotton, felt; 36¼ by 16 by 7 in. Photo: Wendy McEahern. Collection of: Arizona State University Art Museum, Tempe, Arizona

I made a list of quests for humanity and based a series of work upon that list. This vessel is the first in that series. The words "First Quest," "Compassion," and "Mercy" are incorporated into the imagery.

4

5

5

Elaine Small
UNITED STATES

Mysterious Message

Knotted; waxed linen, styrofoam, gesso; 7 by 5 in. Photo: Red Elf

After I have spent hours knotting a linen thread over a core thread to create a basket that isn't intended to contain anything, I think a practical person might doubt my sanity.

6

Peggy Wiedemann
UNITED STATES

Plentiful

Coiled; gourd, pine needles, waxed linen, beads; 8 by 9 by 12 in.

6

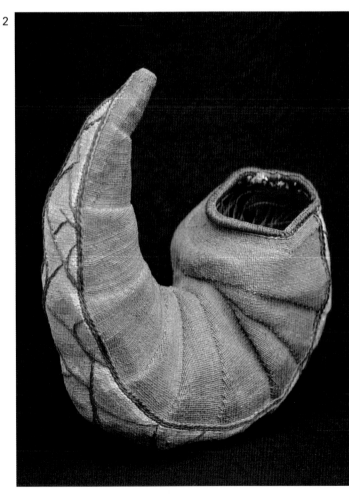

1
Jan Hopkins
UNITED STATES

Five

Stitched, looped, molded, formed; orange peels, lotus pod tops, waxed linen, hemp paper; 5½ by 14¼ by 14½ in. Photo: Jerry McCollum

The number five symbolizes the human microcosm.

2
Kathy Rousso
UNITED STATES

Caminos a las Aldeas

Twined, braided; waxed linen; 10 by 12 by 6 in.

3
Mary M. Miller
UNITED STATES

Waves

Plaited, painted; paper, paint, waxed linen; 4½ by 15 by 5 in.

4
Marilyn Moore
UNITED STATES

Full Bloom

Twined; copper wire and strips, magnet wire; 5½ by 12 by 11 in. Photo: Jerry McCollum

4

5

6

5

Susan Kavicky
United States

Dance of Tides

Plaited; brown ash, yarn; 12 by 18½
in. diameter. Photo: Larry Sanders.

*Long-term relationships require a
tender vigilance, one that recog-
nizes, accepts, and nurtures the inti-
mate connection as well as the
closeness and separateness that is
forever in flux.*

6

Victoria Moran Caluneo
United States

Timeline Series: Personal History

Wrapped, coiled, twist tied, cold con-
nected; copper electrical wire; 8½ by 6½
in. diameter. Photo: Peter San Cherico

1

2

3

1

Cathey Byrd
UNITED STATES

Reds

Coiled, wrapped; pine needles, waxed linen, glass beads; 13 by 6 by 11 in. Photo: Brian Battles

2

Debora Muhl
UNITED STATES

Untitled #1139

Coiled; Maine sweet grass, gourd, nylon ribbon, waxed Irish linen; 11 by 14½ by 12 in. Photo: John Sterling Ruth

3

Karen Simmons
UNITED STATES

Origins

Cast paper; bulb skins, abaca, vine, salt cedar, waxed linen, dye, bone; 35 by 12 by 12 in.
Photo: Margot Geist

I enjoy the opportunity to use bones, feathers, vines, and other materials to amplify the connection between my organic shapes and their inspiration— nests, cocoons, seeds, and pods.

4

4

Danielle Bodine
UNITED STATES

The Guardians

Coiled, assembled; waxed linen, printed mulberry papers, rusted metal brushes, coral, key, bone, porcupine quills; 3 to 8 in. high, 1 to 1 ¾ in. diameter Photo: Bill Jackson

These portable protectors were inspired by the small figures found in Egyptian tombs.

5

Manya Shapiro
UNITED STATES

Vessel

Pieced, pinned; paper, pins; 5 by 7 in. Photo: Bill Bachuber

I enjoy using the materials of daily life to create organic forms which grow as the process unfolds.

6

Liz Stoehr
UNITED STATES

Black Container #3

Plain woven, stitched; braided elastic, thread; 11 by 12 by 29 in. Photo: Bob Elbert

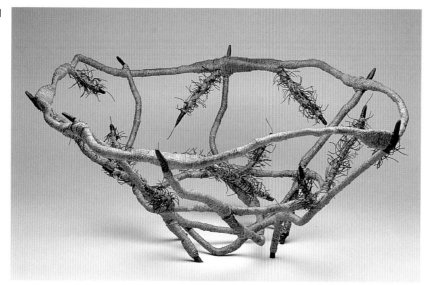

1

Marta Herbertson
AUSTRALIA

Nuts in May

Spun, tied, wrapped; eucalyptus twigs, handspun banana fiber, waxed linen, acrylic paint, beeswax; 11 by 22½ in. diameter.
Photo: Lloyd Hissey

I cannot resist the spent, broken twigs from the eucalypt that fall to the ground. Their shapes dictate what form my work will take.

2

Benjia Morgenstern
UNITED STATES

Basket #23

Woven, interlaced, debarked; Florida grapevine, reed; 9 by 19 by 14 in.
Photo: Don Queralto

I volunteer at a local native preserve where I am permitted to remove Florida native grapevine—but not uproot it—to aid in the control of its rampant growth. I make my baskets from material that would strangle and tip the balance of other native plant life in the park. In helping to keep the balance, I am able to pursue my art.

3

Mark T. Caluneo
UNITED STATES

Curls

Coiled, wrapped; brass, copper, patina; 7 by 8 in. diameter. Photo: Peter San Cherico

The inspiration for this piece came from seeing wood shavings on the floor of a friend's studio. I decided to repeat this one element to capture the beauty of it.

4

Mick Luehrman
UNITED STATES

Somebody Lives Here

Constructed, woven, inked, etched; locust thorn, copper strips, barbed wire; 12 by 14 by 14 in.

This nest-like basket is made from paradoxically inhospitable and impractical materials. As a public-school elementary-art teacher, I was saddened by the realization that more than a few of my students' "nests" were not cozy and warm, but cold and abusive.

4

5

Susan Gutt
UNITED STATES

Set of 3

Plain and twill woven; willow, cane, linseed oil; each piece 38 by 6 by 1 in. Photo: Margot Geist

6

Rod Porco
UNITED STATES

Golden Gourd

Applied gold leaf, woven, fastened; gourd, gold leaf, telephone wire, waxed nylon, glass beads, thorns, grommets; 7 by 12 in. Photo: Tim Brown

7

Sue Boyz
UNITED STATES

Vessel One

Knotless netting, collaged; waxed linen, washi; 3½ by 5 by 5½ in. Photo: Norman Makio

5

6

7

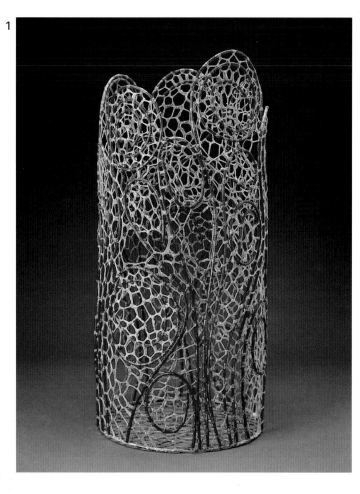

1

Jill Nordfors Clark
UNITED STATES

Koru

Needle-lace basketry; hog casings, dyed reed; 18 by 8½ in. diameter. Photo: Chris Nordfors

2

Briana-Lyn Syvarth
UNITED STATES

Untitled #2

Basketry; steel wire; 14½ by 27 by 15½ in. diameter. Photo: D. James Dee

3

Lindsay K. Rais
UNITED STATES

Stacked Basket

Knotless netting; silver wire, beads, pistachio nut shells, stainless steel mesh; 10 by 8 by 6 in. Photo: D. James Dee

Laboring over mundane objects such as pistachio nut shells, I am able to transform them from something ordinary into something extraordinary.

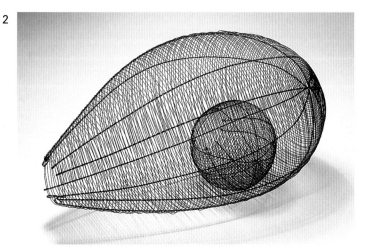

3

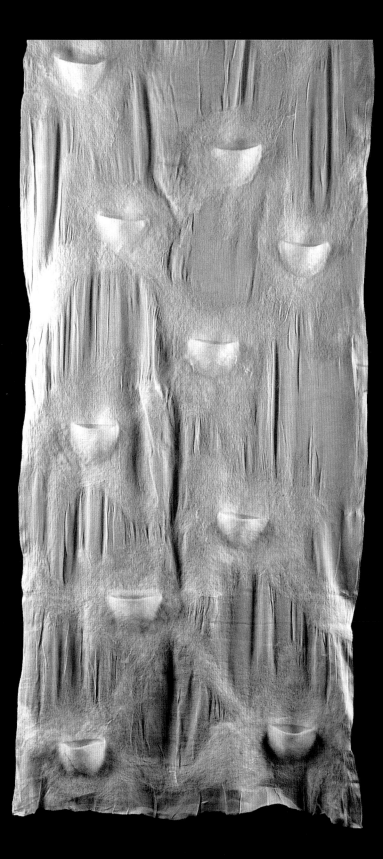

1

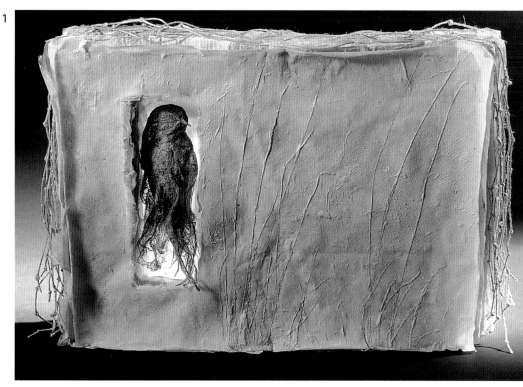

previous page

Frances Dickinson
CANADA

Pockets

Felted; wool, silk; 125 by 44 in.

I want to expand the field of working two dimensionallly on cloth. I like to incorporate techniques that play on the ideas of what defines the nature of cloth.

1

Annie Styron Leonard
UNITED STATES

Untitled

Papermaking, molded, knotted; handmade paper, flax, linen cord, gampi, abaca; 13½ by 10 by 2½ in. Photo: Kate Cameron

My art is informed by the beauty and fragility of the natural world. I use transparent, light fibers such as flax, abaca, and gampi to mold forms and papers which convey a sense of the transitory, ephemeral nature of existence.

2

Andrea Du Flan
UNITED STATES

Morphogenesis

Papermaking, knotless netting; flax, lichen, waxed linen; 12 by 18 by 16 in. Photo: Kate Cameron

2

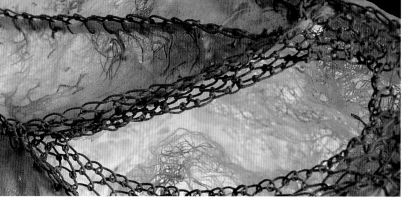

3

5

3

Annie Sherburne
ENGLAND

Soft Cobbles

Felted, sewn; organic undyed fleece, flax, waxed thread; 84 by 72 by 3½ in. Photo: Ed Barber

4

Kathleen Behrens
UNITED STATES

Redwork

Felted, dyed, free-motion machine sewn; merino wool; 28 by 19 in. Photo: Dana Wheelock Photography

This was inspired by the white-on-white needle workers of the 17th and 18th centuries who were forced, through church mandate, from a world of color into a world of color forbidden.

5

Wilma Korenromp
NETHERLANDS

Glacial Flowers

Felted, dyed, embroidered; wool, polyester; 45 by 29½ in.

1

Sue Clancy
UNITED STATES

Yellow Relief

Papermaking, cast paper, pulp painted, embedded; cotton fiber and fabric, pigment; 7 by 8 by ½ in.

3

Judith Pinnell
AUSTRALIA

Bhuj Remembered

Formed-silk paper, appliquéd and reverse appliquéd, machine embroidered, couched; silk paper, metallic fabric and thread; 31 by 23 in.
Photo: Bewley Shaylor

2

Erma Martin Yost
UNITED STATES

Silent Chambers

Felted, dyed, stitched; wool, thread, heat transfer, found object;
12 by 12 in. Photo: Noho Gallery

4

Patricia Spark
UNITED STATES

Oriental Poppies

Needle felted, painted; merino wool, watercolor; 20½ by 18 in.

4

5

6

5

Nicole Chazaud Telaar
UNITED STATES

Wingback Chair

Felted, dyed, inlaid; wool fiber, found chair, dye; 44 by 32 by 32 in. Photo: Dean Powell

6

Erin Endicott
UNITED STATES

Reticent

Painted, collaged, woven; paper, ribbon, vellum, watercolor; 16 by 7 in. Photo: Joseph Hyde

1
Sande French-Stockwell
UNITED STATES

Ancient One
Felted, wrapped, needle felted; wool, polystyrene foam, mixed fibers; 48 by 24 by 16 in.

3
Jennifer Morrow Wilson
UNITED STATES

How does your garden grow?
Hand and machine stitched, collaged, constructed; handmade and commercial paper, wood, copper, waxed linen, tacks, thread, mirror, lamp parts, screening; 36 by 27 by 5 in. Photo: Ken Woisard

2
Jill Powers
UNITED STATES

Planting by the Moon
Cast fiber, stitched; kozo fiber; 17 by 7 by 6 in.

I started cutting seed pods open and was able to see through into the darkness inside, revealing a glimpse into the place where the seeds grow and contain their energetic potential. The seed's coming to life is a sacred process, and one which we do not usually get to witness.

3

4

4

Jo Stealey
UNITED STATES

Shrine

Papermaking, coiled, cast; flax, honey-locust thorns, waxed linen, embroidery floss, wood; 18 by 8 by 2½ in. Photo: Peter Anger

This piece is a shrine to woman as vessel. The thorns that are poked inside the bottom vessel and around the openings of the niches are representative of the "little pricks of life."

5

Grimanesa Amoros
UNITED STATES

Fotomana: African Housing

Papermaking; cotton pulp, clay, straw, sand; 30 by 48 in. Photo: Eric Guttelewitz

In 1994, I obtained an NEA grant and an Arts International traveling grant to visit Ghana and the Ivory Coast. The trip lasted two months. In the small, tourist-free villages, I found a world that enchanted me with its spiritual and natural integrity and met people oblivious to many Western anxieties.

5

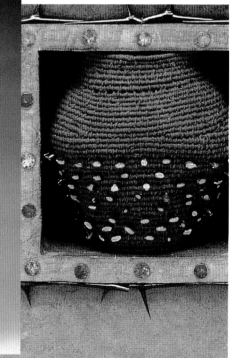

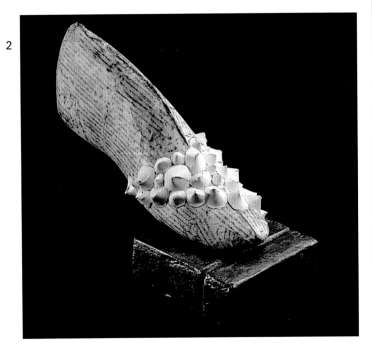

1
Rachel Starr Suntop
UNITED STATES

Pods

Papermaking, sculpted, glued; kozo and gampi fiber, glue; largest piece 13 by 13 by 13 in. Photo: Larry Gawel

2
Judith Ingram
UNITED STATES

Toeing the Line #7

Papermaking, cast, collaged, glued, rubbed, painted; paper pulp, rice paper, graphite, acrylic paint; 7½ by 9 by 3¼ in. Photo: Rick Echelmeyer

3
Bird Ross
UNITED STATES

Accordion Cone

Machine stitched; nautical maps, handmade paper, thread; 10 by 14 by 9 in. Photo: Bill Lemke

The maps became the focal point of this vessel series where I explored the metamorphosis of a two-dimensional plane into a three-dimensional object.

4
Sabine Thornau
GERMANY

Schalen (Bowls)

Papermaking, dyed, formed; cotton cellulose, pigments; 50 by 125 in. Photo: Jürgen Hohl

To me, bowls and receptacles mean body, room, content, contact between interior and exterior, skin, cover, protection.

3

4

5

5

Heather Kerner
UNITED STATES

Earth Song

Felted, coiled, lashed; wool batts, aluminum wire, leather cord, twig; 12 by 10 in diameter. Photo: Lizarri Photographic

6

Julie McLaughlin
UNITED STATES

Preying Mantis

Papermaking, constructed; flax, abaca, linen fiber, steel-rod armature; 21 by 17½ by 8½ in.

Years of creating costumes for the theatre have evolved into a more personal creative journey using handmade paper. I use abaca and flax fibers, highly beaten, which have a high shrinkage rate as they dry, creating an unusual visual experience when stretched over steel-rod corset armatures.

6

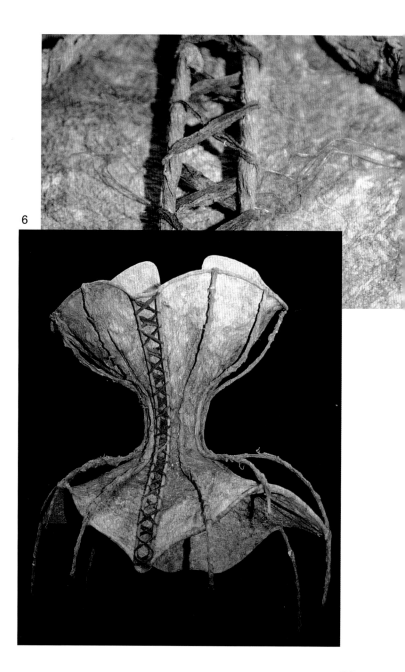

1

Clare Diprose
ENGLAND

Florence

Felted, dyed; merino wool, dye; 17 by 11 in.

I am drawn to skylines, patterns of light on water, the turn of a head or hand—brief fragmentary visions that enrich the mundane.

2

Bronwyn Hunter
AUSTRALIA

Sea Creatures Crawling

Felted, dyed; cotton voile, Australian merino wool. Australian dye; 115 by 10 in. Photo: Ian Johnson

This is my first and favorite Nuno-felted piece—pieces of merino wool felted directly onto cotton fabric, then hand dyed. I love to work with organic shapes, and color is one of my passions.

3

Manya Shapiro
UNITED STATES

Altar

Collaged, pinned; paper, pins; 18 by 21 in. Photo: Bill Bachuber

4

Linelle Dickinson
UNITED STATES

Armor Sapien

Shifu (woven cloth of paper), stitched, dyed, discharged, knotted; paper thread weft, cotton thread warp, dress-pattern paper, dye. Photo: Michael J. Walter

This piece is a metaphor of the many defensive layers we put up against our surroundings.

4

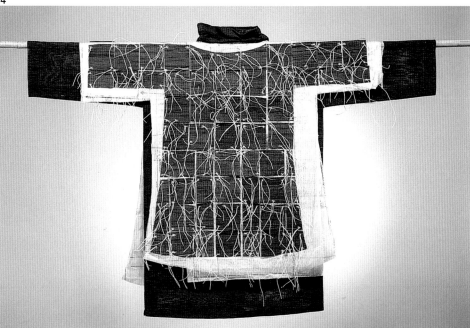

5

5

Erica Spitzer Rasmussen
UNITED STATES

Dirty Little Secret

Cast paper; flax, acrylics, wax, horsehair; 48 by 64 by 42 in. Photo: P. Ytsma

At the beginning of the 20th century, it was discovered that exposure to x rays could be used as an effortless and painless form of depilating unwanted body and facial hair. In the years that followed, many women were diagnosed with radiation-induced cancer. I found the disastrous result to be a poignant example of how destructive the pursuit of feminine beauty can be in our physically obsessed society.

6

Barbara McCaffrey
CANADA

Fault Line

Felted, hand dyed, pieced, embroidered; wool, dye, silk thread. 44 by 44 in. Photo: Janet Dwyer

Living on an island in the Pacific Northwest has its faults!

3

1

2

4

1

Patricia Zobel Canaday
UNITED STATES

Grid IV

Papermaking, sprayed, photo transfer; paper pulp, wooden grid, photos; 43 by 33 by 2 in. Photo: C. Belton

2

Robert Forman
UNITED STATES

Birth

Glued; cotton, linen, silk, and rayon thread, backing board, glue; 36 by 24 in. Photo: Jeff Goldman

3

Anne Taylor
UNITED STATES

Busy Hands

Papermaking, collaged, drawn; handmade paper, commercial paper; 12½ by 15½ in.

4

Ellen A. Petersen
UNITED STATES

Tale of Tears

Drawn, painted, beaded; handmade paper, ink, acrylic paint, bleach; 34 by 26 in.

5

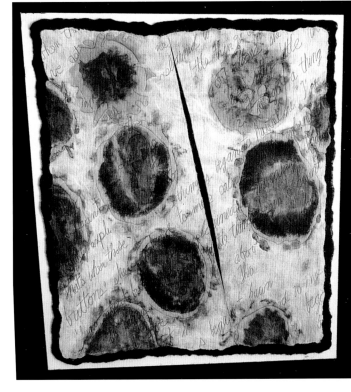

5
Cecilia Voss Eager
UNITED STATES

She's Got a Thing About Buttons

Felted, machine stitched; wool;
42 by 47 in.

6a front
6b back

Kelly Mulloy
UNITED STATES

Blue-Yellow-Red

Felted, machine stitched; raw and
hand-dyed merino and mohair-blend
wool, thread; 84 by 36 in.
Photo: Artworks

7
Renee Harris
UNITED STATES

Windshift

Hand felted and embroidered; wool
and cotton thread; 26 by 30 in.
Photo: C. W. Schauer

8
Sylvia Whitesides
UNITED STATES

Friends

Felted, dyed, pieced, hand stitched;
dye, wool, cotton, perle cotton; 15½
by 13 in.

7

6a

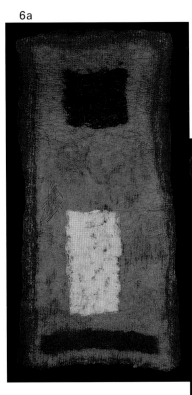

6b

8

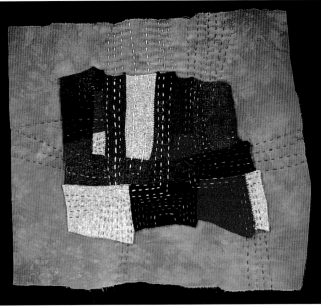

1

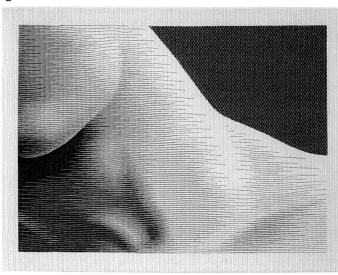

2

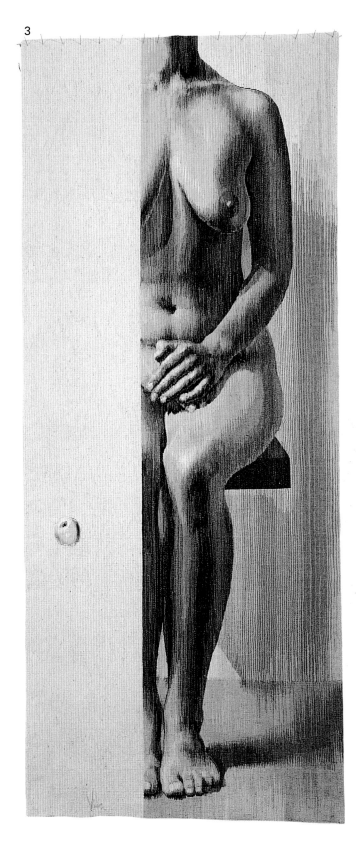

3

opposite page

Ainsley Hillard
WALES

Reminiscence, Series #3

Tapestry, photography, heat transfer; monofilament warp, printed-viscose yarn weft, acrylic, cotton, lead; three panels, 98 by 25½ in, 108 by 25½ in, and 94 by 25½ in.
Photo: Robert Frith

1

Archie Brennan
UNITED STATES

Drawing Series XLIV: Study

Tapestry; cotton warp, raw silk, wool, and cotton weft; 22¼ by 11¼ in.

2

Tim Gresham
AUSTRALIA

Rest

Flat-woven tapestry; wool, cotton; 24½ by 32 in.

This study of a neck is part of a series looking at details of the body.

3

Vita Geluniene
LITHUANIA

Two Bodies

Gobelin tapestry; flax, wool, cotton; 74 by 34 in. Photo: G. Cesonis

1

2

3

4

5

6

1

Aase Vaslow
UNITED STATES

This is Not the Real Me

Beaded tapestry, loom woven, mounted; linen, seed beads; 7 by 5 in. Photo: Mignon Naegeli

2

Priscilla Lynch
UNITED STATES

Proof of Identity

Gobelin tapestry; cotton warp, wool weft; 25 by 25 in.

After my wallet and all my identification were stolen, I started thinking of how we prove our identity—photo, fingerprint, numbers, DNA profile—none of which tell anyone who we really are.

3

Teresa Graham Salt
UNITED STATES

Middle-age Panic

Tapestry; silk buttonhole-twist thread; 8 by 6 in.

4

Kathy Spoering
UNITED STATES

Croquet Coquette

Tapestry; wool weft on cotton warp; 53 by 36 in.

5

Janita Loder
UNITED STATES

You're in the Army Now!

Tapestry, painted, hand dyed; wool weft, cotton warp, fabric paint, dye; 15 by 15 in.

The inspiration for this piece was a family photo and memories of my children when they were young.

6

Tori S. Kleinert
UNITED STATES

Terroristic Semblance: Destruction of the Fold

Small-format tapestry; linen, cotton; 9 by 10 in. Photo: J. M. Kleinert

1
Barbara Heller
CANADA

French Foreign Legionnaires
Tapestry, dyed; linen warp, wool weft; 39 by 32 in.

I am exploring the way we relate to people whose faces are covered up by their clothing or costume. There is tension as we strive to make eye contact but cannot. Often the body language belies the interpretation we put on the costume, and so we misjudge.

2
Sarah Swett
UNITED STATES

Escape Literature
Flat tapestry, two-sided, weft-faced plain weave; wool warp, wool weft, natural dyes; 48 by 36 in.
Photo: Mark LaMoreaux

3

4

3

Shelley Socolofsky
United States

Well of Surrender

Gobelin tapestry; wool, silk, cotton;
84 by 60 in. Photo: Ken Altman

4

Kaija Rautiainen
Canada

Sense of Earth

Tapestry; wool warp, linen and wool
weft; 36 by 31 in.

5

Christine Sawyer
England

Journey

Gobelin tapestry; wool, cotton;
63 by 60 in. Photo: David Sawyer

6

Renata Rozsívalová
Czech Republic

Diachrony of Quadrate

Tapestry combined with relief loops;
cotton warp, wool weft; 106 by 77 in.
Photo: Jaroslav Rajzík

5

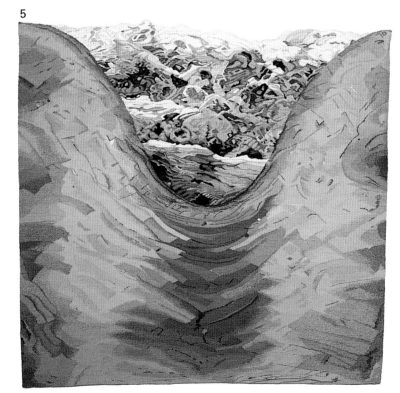

6

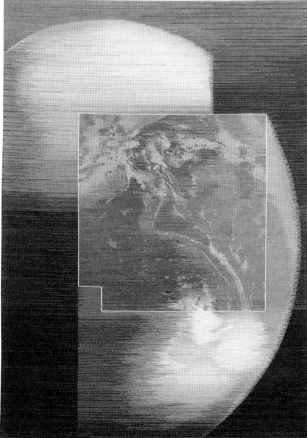

1

Mary Kester
UNITED STATES

Brittany Portal

Tapestry, layered; wool, cotton; 72 by 69 by 4 in. Photo: Cindi Bell

2

Cecilia Blomberg
UNITED STATES

Rowing Vérité

Flat tapestry; cotton-seine twine warp, wool and linen weft; 21 by 32 in.

I row with a group of women in a wooden gig—a replica of a French admiral's barge—with 10 oars, each 18 feet long, one per rower.

3

Nancy Jackson
UNITED STATES

Cypress

Gobelin/Aubusson tapestry; wool on cotton warp; 42¾ by 61 in. Photo: Nancy Jackson

4

Susan Kelli
CANADA

Exchanges

Tapestry; wool, cotton, rayon; 15 by 15 in.

This tapestry ponders the exchanges people make in life. Layers of meaning in the symbols from games, tarot cards, and the measures of time reflect the many dimensions of human experience.

4

7

5

6

5

Bobbi Chamberlain
UNITED STATES

Devil's Bridge 1

Tapestry; cotton warp, wool weft; 46 by 60 in.

In today's fast-paced society, it is refreshing to work in an art form that has changed little in centuries.

6

Ruth Collier Manning
UNITED STATES

How Long Does it Take to Clean it Up?

Slit tapestry; wool, cotton; 36 by 48 in.
Photo: Andy Olenick

I became interested in the relativity of time after years of answering the question we hear most often, "How long did it take to weave that piece?" I've yet to give an accurate answer—longer than some things you do, but perhaps not as long as others.

7

Pacific Rim Tapestries
UNITED STATES

Labyrinth

Tapestry with floating weft; wool weft, cotton warp;
60 by 60 in. Photo: Cecilia Blomberg

Pacific Rim Tapestries is a collaborative studio combining the talents of Cecilia Blomberg, Mary Lane, and Margo Macdonald. Labyrinth is their second tapestry.

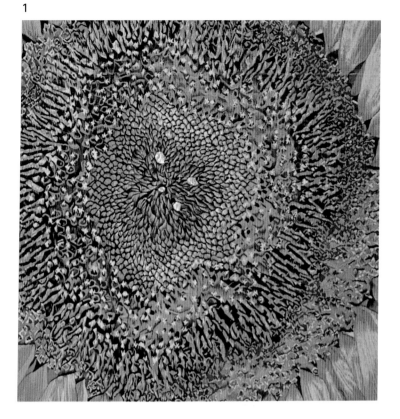

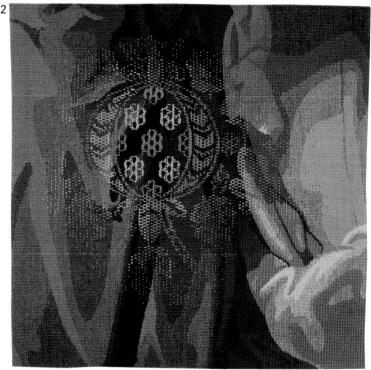

1

Tricia Goldberg
UNITED STATES

Sunflower

Tapestry, slit woven, double-weft interlock, color blended; wool, cotton, silk, 72 by 72 in. Photo: Margaret Williams

2

Murray Gibson
UNITED STATES

Visitation

Gobelin tapestry; wool and cotton on cotton warp; 24 by 24 in. Collection of: Cambridge Galleries, Cambridge, Ontario, Canada

3

Mary-Alice Huemoeller
UNITED STATES

"Thangka"

Woven, painted warp, soumak laid-in wrapping; rayon warp, cotton weft, dye; 88 by 51 in. Photo: David Swift

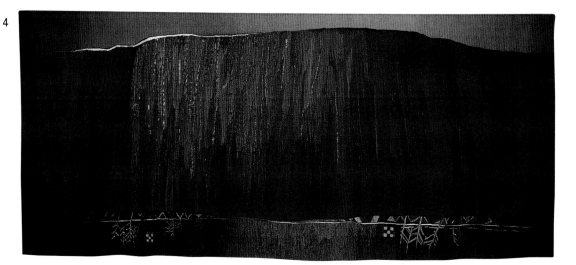

4

Irisa Blumate
Latvia

Australia

Tapestry; wool, synthetics, linen;
67 by 150 in.

5

Kari Guddal
Denmark

When Shadows are Shining

Haute lisse; Norwegian spelsau wool
on flax warp; 118½ by 79½ in.
Photo: Torben Dragsby

6

Karen Benjamin
United States

Southwest Sunrise

Tapestry; hand-dyed wool on cotton
warp; each panel 30 by 156 in.
Photo: Dan Morse

*This commissioned work was my
favorite opportunity for color play.*

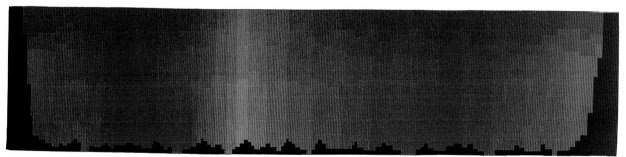

3

1
Cygan Wlodzimierz
POLAND

I Know Where I Came From

Tapestry, converging warp; linen, polypropylene; 71 by 102 in. Photo: Lech and Rzedewski

2
Inge Norgaard
UNITED STATES

The Song of the Ocean

Free-style Gobelin tapestry; cotton warp, wool weft; 52 by 56 inches. Photo: C. Haniford

3
Aija Baumane
LATVIA

Time VI

Tapestry; wool, linen, synthetics; 73 by 83 in.

4
Emmajo Webster
SCOTLAND

Trades of Ayr

Tapestry; wool, cotton, silk; 36 by 84 in.
Photo: Keith Hunter Photography

This tapestry was woven as part of a residency for South Ayrshire Council. The tapestry was woven in public at London Hall, one of the oldest trades houses in Ayr.

4

1

Suzanne Pretty
United States

Forest of Blocks

Single-interlock tapestry; wool, silk, cotton, metallics; 44½ by 56 in. Photo: Andrew Edgar

As a child plays with blocks, we toy with our environment, arranging and rearranging. Blocks of forest create little isolated environments cut off with strips of land turned desolate with chemicals and paving. Migrating animal populations are unable to move freely across the landscape. Vehicles pollute the air in and around the isolated blocks.

2

Susan Martin Maffei
United States

Traffic N.Y.C. 2001

Gobelin tapestry; wool, cotton, linen, silk, mixed fibers; 80 by 48 in.

4

6

5

3

Anne Jackson
ENGLAND

Old Master II

Knotted tapestry; cotton, linen, synthetics; 36 by 30 in. Photo: Pete Merrett

My work often comments on the state of the world and the place of women in it. A frequent theme is the male nude, turning the tables just a little bit.

4

Lilla C. Roberts
UNITED STATES

Wedding Rings

Tapestry; cotton-seine twine warp, wool weft; 48 by 36 in.

5

Karen Page Crislip
UNITED STATES

Sweet Light on Sandstone

High-warp Gobelin tapestry; cotton warp, wool weft; 21 ¼ by 21 ½ in.

I depict the movement of light and seasons across stone striations by the juxtaposition of color using a southwest tapestry technique of outlining to produce elongated and undulating shapes.

6

Kristin Carlsen Rowley
UNITED STATES

Bonnie's Millefleurs

Tapestry; hand-dyed wool yarn on wool warp; 78 by 46 in.
Photo: Pat Pollard

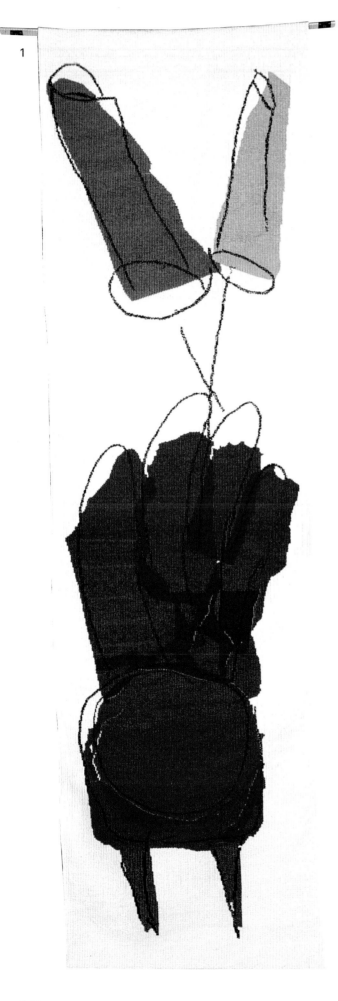

1

2

3

4

5

6

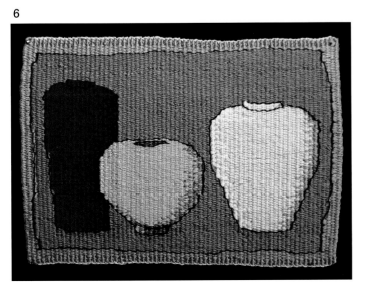

1

Thomas Cronenberg
GERMANY

*Heimweh
(Missing Home)*
Gobelin tapestry; linen warp, wool
and silk weft; 138½ by 39½ in.
Photo: Anja Burmeister

2

Elinor Steele
UNITED STATES

Five Chairs
High-warp tapestry; wool on cotton
warp; 51 by 18 in.

3

Helga Berry
UNITED STATES

Becoming Predestined
Tapestry; wool, silk, metallic and
synthetic fiber; 68 by 68 in.
Photo: Chris Arend Photography

4

Laurie Dill-Kocher
UNITED STATES

The Path of the Ladder
Tapestry; cotton warp, wool weft;
66 by 168 in. Photo: Thomas Kocher

My approach to any work is a celebration of the visual tension that I
can create through dyeing,
coloring, or manipulation of the
material.

5

Susan Iverson
UNITED STATES

Horizon: Dreaming Sacsahuaman
Tapestry with pulled warp; linen, silk;
24 by 63 by 3 in. Photo: Taylor
Dabney

*This tapestry was inspired by memo-
ries of the pre-Columbian fortress
near Cuzco, Peru.*

6

Joy Smith
AUSTRALIA

Vases x 3
Tapestry; cotton warp and weft; 4 by
5½ in. Photo: Douglas Willis

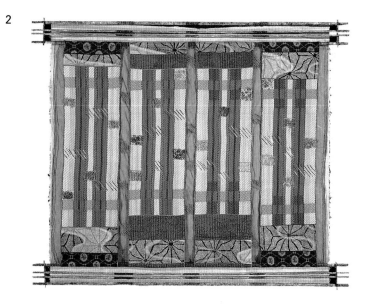

1

Care Standley
UNITED STATES

Crone Eggs

Tapestry; wool, cotton, silk; 18 by 24 in. Photo: Kim Harrington

2

Cameron Taylor-Brown
UNITED STATES

Layers of Meaning

Woven, pieced, painted, stitched; linen, rayon, cotton, wood, paper, nylon mesh; 38 by 48 in. Photo: "Q"

3

Charlotte Ziebarth
UNITED STATES

Houses on the Hillside

Slit tapestry; wool, cotton, and silk weft, cotton warp; 55 by 38 in.

I love leaves. I quilt them, print them, draw them, photograph them, scan them, bead them, and weave them.

4

Audrey Moore
UNITED STATES

The Ladies Series II

Navajo tapestry; hand-dyed wool, shells; 34 by 31 in.
Photo: Dennis Purdy

4

5

Deborah Corsini
UNITED STATES

Flashback

Navajo wedge-woven tapestry; cotton warp, wool weft; 40 by 30 in.

The deep jewel tones reflect an atmosphere, and the zigzag lines create an electric charge. Is this a psychedelic experience, a vision of the Amazon jungle, or some unknown energy field? I hope my work stirs other memories and interpretations.

6

Jay Wilson
UNITED STATES

Blue Diamonds

Tapestry; wool and linen; 78 by 48 in.
Photo: Joe Higgins

5

6

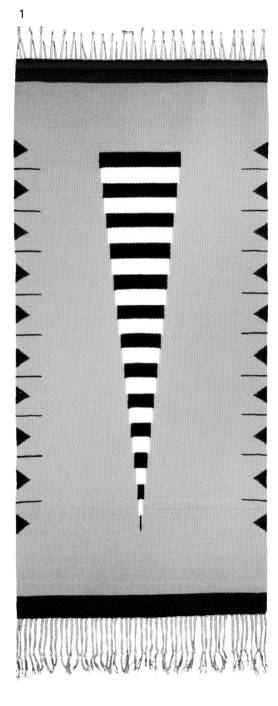

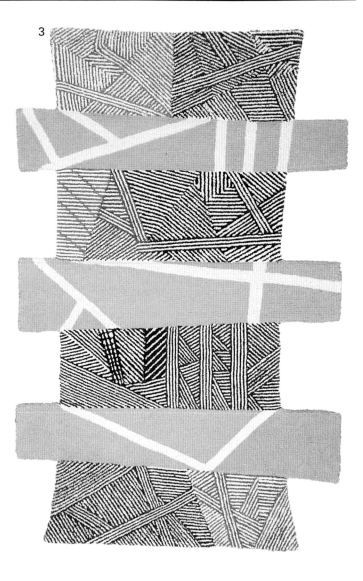

1

Mary Zicafoose
UNITED STATES

Twister with Stripes

Slit-woven tapestry; wool on linen warp; 74 by 36 in.
Photo: Kirby Zicafoose

This piece combines my three favorite elements of graphic tapestry design: use of an archetypal symbol, creation of a large saturated color field, and rhythm through high-contrast repetitive stripes.

2

James Koehler
UNITED STATES

Aspen View

Tapestry; hand-dyed wool and silk weft, cotton warp; 28 by 56 in.
Photo: James Hart

I am influenced by the extraordinary landscape and the unique cultures of New Mexico and by an aesthetic of simplicity, purity, and portraying only what is essential.

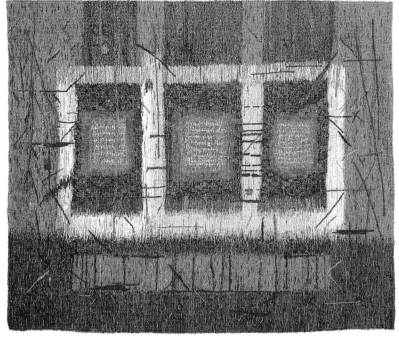

4

6

5

3
Martha Donovan Opdahl
United States

Arroyo Seco #1

Tufted, dyed, wool pile, cotton backing, acid dyes, punch gun; 78 by 53 in. Photo: Dan Morse

The formal elements of my work are metaphors for life's spontaneity, randomness, and lyricism, as well as its constraints, predictability, and order.

4
Ann Schumacher
United States

Chaos/Silence

Tapestry, embroidered; wool, rayon, silk, embroidery thread; 30 by 37 in. Photo: Mary Rezny

5
Gudrun Pagter
Denmark

Sense of Space I

Gobelin/flat-woven tapestry; wrap seaming, dyed-sisal weft; 87 by 75 in. Photo: Poulsen Fotografi

6
Joanne Cromley
United States

Jewel Point

Tapestry; cotton, hand-dyed wool; 48 by 35 in. Photo: John Wooden

Each tapestry I weave is designed to express simple, sharp, clean, geometric images via precision-weaving techniques. Through color and design, I hope emotions are evoked that take the viewer to an abstract concept and place.

107

fiber sculpture
&
installations

opposite page

Naoko Serino
JAPAN

Existing

Molded; jute string; 7 by 7 by 7 in.

1

Nancy Ziegler Nodelman
UNITED STATES

Tome

Deconstructed, painted, patinated, assembled, mounted; books, acrylics, pigments; 9 by 13 by 3 in.
Photo: Hap Sakwa

2

Jason Ripper
UNITED STATES

Shadow (self portrait)

Twined, sewn; commercial fabric, cotton balls, thread; 84¼ by 27¼ by 2 in. Photo: Damian Johnson

3

Marty Jonas
UNITED STATES

Split Image

Pleated, hand stitched and embroidered; dyed cotton, silk thread, wire frame; 18 by 13 by 4 in. Photo: Hedi Desuyo

This wonderful fabric, when pleated, reminds me of tree bark. The process of manipulating fibers into figurative sculptures is a technical challenge.

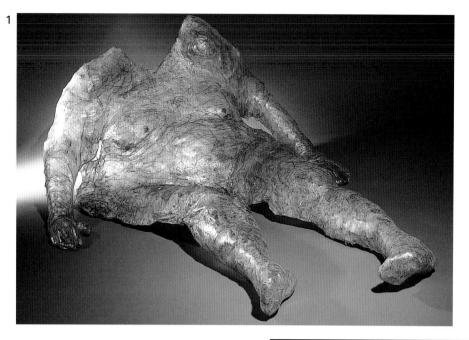

1

Sara Gordon
UNITED STATES

Today's Venus

Constructed; gut, plastic; 22 by 47 by
51 in. Photo: Kate Cameron

*For the last year and a half, I have
been creating life-sized, middle-aged,
large women, all beautiful, wonderful, and all based on real people. My
goal is to communicate the magnifi-
cence and the vulnerability of these
women. I want to tell the story of a
woman's life experience.*

2

Judy Bales
UNITED STATES

Embracing Hills

Wrapped, painted; cotton, wire,
acrylic paint; 19 by 37 by 15 in.
Photo: Jerry Anthony

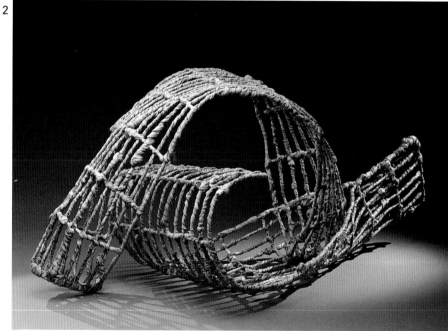

4

5

6

3

Karen Urbanek
UNITED STATES

Leaf Tumbler I
Dyed, layered, manipulated, coated; silk, polymer medium, waxed linen, apple twigs; 17 by 28 by 25 in. Photo: Don Tuttle Photography

4

Jan Hopkins
UNITED STATES

Within

Stitched, looped, molded, formed; agave leaves, Alaskan yellow cedar bark, waxed linen; 6½ by 13 by 13 in. Photo: Jerry McCollum

5

Kristin L. Tollefson
UNITED STATES

Bright Mound

Soumak, woven, stitched, constructed; steel wire, plastic pearls; 9 by 15 by 15 in.

I am a metalsmith with fiber tendencies. Utilizing traditional fiber techniques of stitching and weaving, I build my work out of metal wire and surplus, cast off, or industrial materials.

6

Susan Etcoff Fraerman
UNITED STATES

Alteration

Off-loom bead woven, manipulated; cotton, thermoplastic, glass seed beads, pigment, nylon thread, linen; 15 by 9 by 10 in. Photo: Tom Van Eynde

This piece was inspired by the courage, resilience, and beauty of a breast-cancer survivor.

1

3

2

1

Judy L. Kahle
UNITED STATES

Controlled Anger

Machine stitched, collaged;
thread, blueprinted cotton,
canvas; 13 by 9 by 3 in.
Photo: Jerry Anthony

*Color tells the story on this
vessel. The calm blues and vio-
lets can barely contain the hot
yellows and oranges coming
from within the inner form.*

2

Barbara Lee Smith
UNITED STATES

Tumbling Blocks 1-5

Painted, fused, stitched, melt-
ed; synthetic fabric, acrylic
paint, wood; 33 to 44 in. high.
Photo: Tom Holt

*These pieces balance some-
where between strength and
vulnerability. "Tumbling
Blocks," a series of sculptures,
are purposefully not quite
upright. To my mind, they
show some ravages of time,
but still stand with a sense of
purpose, even if it's to provide
a memory.*

4

5

3

Susan Taber Avila
UNITED STATES

Jubilance

Stitched; thread; 18 by 8 by 5 in.
Photo: Philip Cohen

4

Margot Van Lindenberg
CANADA

Chromosomes

Felted, embroidered; wool, foam,
wire, beads, embroidery floss; each
17 by 3½ in. diameter.

5

Jean Jones
UNITED STATES

Bamboo Pages

Woven, supplementary weft, painted, wrapped; bamboo-yarn warp and
weft, bamboo sticks, Thai paper, silk;
open view 6 by 72 in., closed view 6
by 6¾ by 2½ in. Photo: Dan Morse

6

Susan Stone
UNITED STATES

The Three Magi

Knotted, braided; elk bones, metallic
thread, tribal beads, wrought iron
stands; each 14 by 3 by 4 in.
Photo: Garth Dowling

6

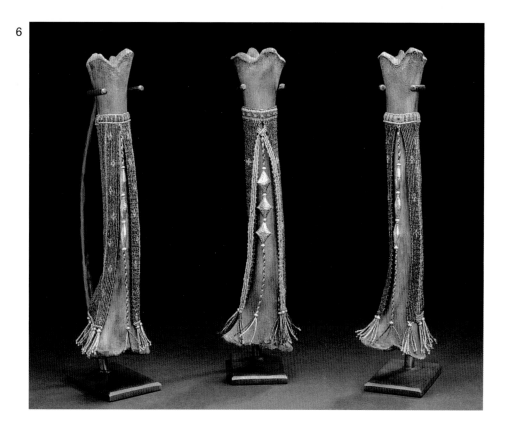

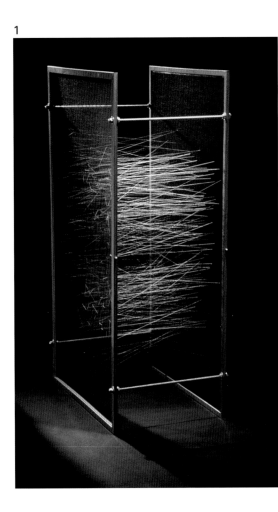

1

Randy Walker
UNITED STATES

Two Planes

Threaded; aluminum window screens, nylon thread; 36 by 12 in. Photo: Doug Deutscher

2

Fran Reed
UNITED STATES

Snapper Charm

Stitched; red snapper skin, gut, willow, wishbones, telephone wire; 15 by 24 by 18 in. Photo: Chris Arend

Wicked fins, but loaded with good luck.

2

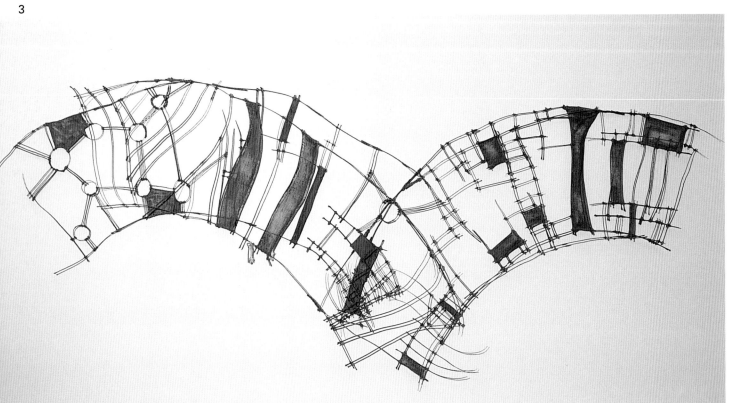

3

4

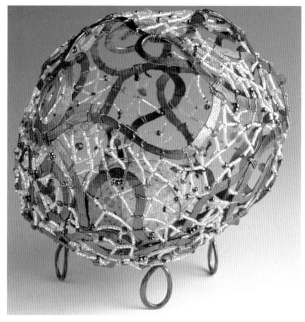

5

3

Melissa Hirsch
AUSTRALIA

Span

Constructed; jacaranda wood,
muslin, earth; 36 by 114 in.

4

Cindy Wrobel
UNITED STATES

Calm in the Eye of a Storm

Wrapped, hammered, beaded,
woven; copper wire, beads, rock; 8
by 8 by 7 in. Photo: Jim Sokolik

5

Jóh Ricci
UNITED STATES

Organized Chaos

Eccentric half-hitch and double half-
hitch knotted; nylon twine, rocks,
sphere; diameter 3 in.

6

Jane Whitten
AUSTRALIA

Untitled

Knitted, sculpted; cotton yarn, sand,
baling wire, rock, glue; 20 by 24 by
11 in. Photo: Julian Beveridge

6

1

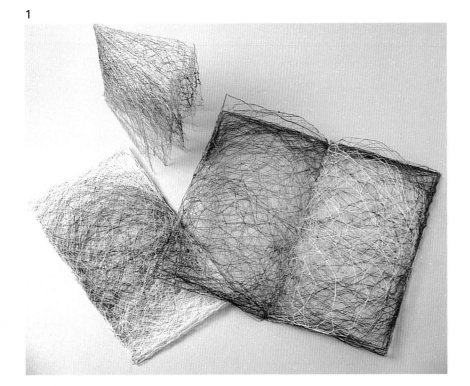

1

Teresa Pla Belio
SPAIN

Textile Books

Plaited; cotton; 6 by 4 in., 13 by 8 in.,
13 by 8 in. Photo: Jordi Balanya

These three books belong to a col-
lection. I have tried to "write" with
colors and transparency, so this is
very important in my work as well as
to create austere forms.

2

Miyuki Akai
UNITED STATES

Behind the Twin Towers

Cyanotype, quilted; cotton, yarn,
wood, metal springs; 17 by 13 in.
Photo: Jonathan Reynolds

2

3

4

5

3

Aafke Stavenga
NETHERLANDS

About a Good Time

Tied, painted, printed, folded; silk, rubber, hemp, toothpicks, linen; 50 by 40 by 2½ in.

4

Natasha St. Michael
CANADA

Ferment

Peyote-stitch beadwoven; glass beads, nylon thread, metal support; 6½ by 23½ by 19½ in.
Photo: Paul Litherland

5

Li-Chih Wang
TAIWAN

999 Rose

Sewn, screen printed; rose branch, artificial silk.

It's a love story. Love is forever.

1

1

Donna Rhae Marder
United States

Breakthrough

Machine sewn, formed; 35mm
slides, wire, metallic thread; 18 by 20
by 12 in. Photo: Dean Powell

2

Georgette L. Veeder
United States

Evolution of the Woolly Bully

Felted, needlefelted; wool fleece;
35 by 35 by 5 in.

2

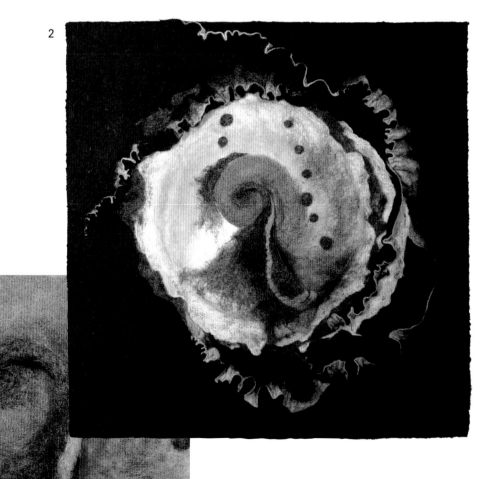

3

3

Donna Kallner
UNITED STATES

Grass Slipper

Coiled, needleworked; Siberian iris leaves, Irish linen, shoe; 5¼ by 10 by 3½ in.

I grew up in a time and place where ladies wore high-heeled shoes with narrow toes. And oh, how lovely they made your legs look! But the shoes outlasted the feet in our culture and left a legacy of hammer toes, calluses, bunions, and fallen arches.

4

Carol Durham
UNITED STATES

Urban Runner

Layered, cut, painted, glued; hog casings, polystyrene foam, cotton balls; 7 by 10 by 6 in. Photo: Gugger Petter

5

Jane Sauer
UNITED STATES

Endear/Endure

Knotted; waxed linen, gourds, pigment; 18 by 10 by 14 in. Photo: Wendy McEahern

4

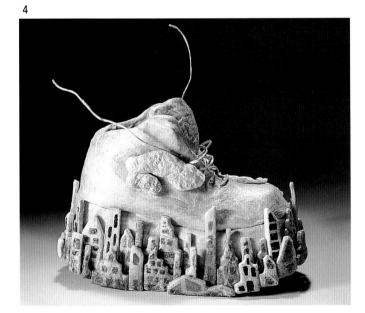

5

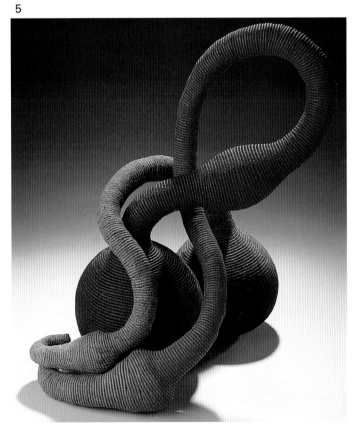

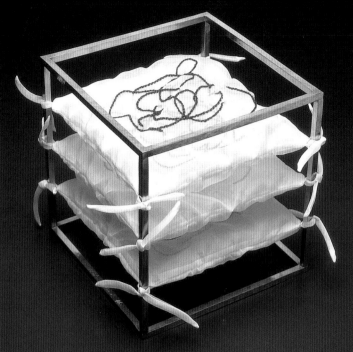

1

Akiko Kotani
UNITED STATES

Floating Pillows

Drawn, stitched; silk thread, silk
organza, pewter; 8 by 8 by 8 in.
Photo: Joseph Rudinec

*The most elemental artistic gesture
of all, the drawn line on a surface,
issues from the use of silk threads
stitched on layers of silk organza.
The lingering evanescence of feeling
results from the multiple layering.*

2

Sugane Hara
JAPAN

The Shore/Dialogue

Machine stitched; fabric, thread.
Photo: Mareo Suemasa

*Standing beside the shore and think-
ing, we look different, we are quite different, but does it have some important meaning? We breathe the same
way, we utter the same way, and we
can hear each other's voice in the
same way. We don't need conflct any-
more. We only need dialogue like
calm waves. Now waves come to the
shore so calm; a man is standing
beyond the sea. He is not the enemy,
he is our partner for this dialogue.*

2

3

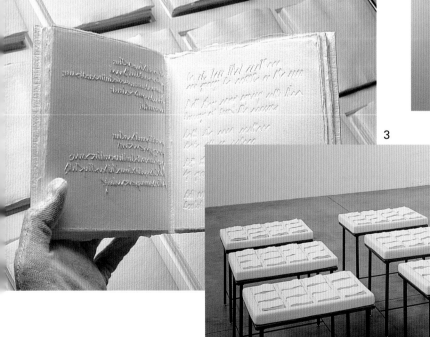

4

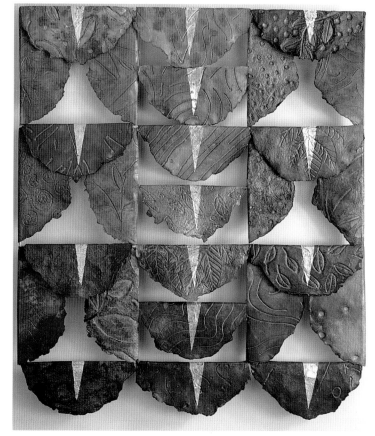

6

5

3

Linda Welker
UNITED STATES

Navigation (Text)

Bookmaking, stitched, pierced, letterpress, cast, incised; handmade paper, handspun-silk thread, plaster, stainless steel; 2¾ by 16 by 17 ft. Photo: Brian McLernon

4

Priscilla Robinson
UNITED STATES

27 Resting Butterflies II

Embossed, dried, painted; golden acrylic, cotton, Phillipine abaca, white gold leaf; 42 by 36 by 2 in.

5

Barbara Setsu Pickett
UNITED STATES

Recover Book IV

Woven, textblock sewn; silk thread, silk organza, Indian metallic cloth, bead; 3 by 3 by¾ in. Photo: Richard Gehrke

6

Akemi Cohn
UNITED STATES

Broken Circle #B

Hand painted, hand dyed, appliquéd, constructed; silk, polyester, aluminum bars, steel, wood, fabric fasteners; 86 by 68 by 24 in.

In my work, I use a traditional Japanese rice-paste resist-printing technique called Nassen.

1

2

1
Sherri Wood
UNITED STATES

Hot Ass Baby

Hand embroidered; found dolls, cotton embroidery floss, tattoo (designed by Denise de la Cerde); 18-in. doll. Photo: Bill Gage

This is from the "The Tattoo Baby Doll Project," a collaboration with female tattoo artists from across the country that combines embroidery and tattoo as a way to explore the shifting images and roles that define and empower women today.

2
Lucy G. Feller
UNITED STATES

A Child's War Dress

Photo transfer, stitched, embroidered; American flag, christening dress, buttons, ribbons, photos, rhinestones, stars; 31 by 22 by 3 in. Photo: D. James Dee

3
Mary Giehl
UNITED STATES

Inner Light of Children

Sewn; muslin, beeswax, cherry wood hangers; each 32 by 22 by 4 in. Photo: David Moore

4
Meredith Ré Grimsley
UNITED STATES

Identity

Machine sewn, embossed; cotton-rag tracing paper, thread, shredded paper, wire hangers, blue dryer sheets; 8 by 68 by 10 ft.

3

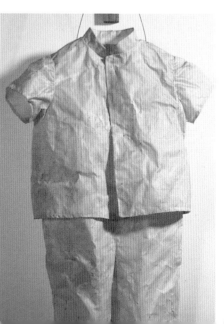

4

5

6

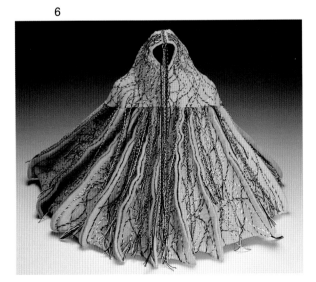

5
Ruth Seider
UNITED STATES

Sacred Path

Screen printed, free-motion machine embroidered, hand-woven, dextrin resist, discharged, knitted, indigo dyed; linen, silk, rayon, copper wire, nylon rope, thorns, lace, canvas, shredded book, screening. Photo: Bill Lemke

My work is based on the Medieval cope with prominent use of the labyrinth as part of the design. This work is about the sacred path that we all walk in our everyday lives.

6
Barbara Schulman
UNITED STATES

Enigmatologist

Embroidered, pieced, constructed; industrial wool felt, linen thread; 15 by 22½ by 20 in. Photo: Jeff Unger

My work is about identity, depicted as powerful, protective, healing, or magical female figures. My hand-stitched and braided patterns are evocative of woven fabric.

1

Meghan Lancaster
UNITED STATES

Circle

Stenciled, paste resist, dyed, overdyed, cut, folded, sewn; cotton scrim, rebar, cardboard, stones, feathers, shell, wood, reactive dye; 90 by 84 in. diameter.

2

Lee Renninger
UNITED STATES

Curtain

High fired, hand cut, glazed, knotted; porcelain clay, celadon glaze, cotton crochet thread; 11 by 8 ft.

My work is primarily clay-based but often incorporates other media and found objects in an installation format. This particular body of work explores clay as fabric. The translucency of high-fired porcelain is much like that of fine, sheer fabric. The light penetrates but is filtered and diffused. The shadows form yet another layer of fabric, although an illusory one.

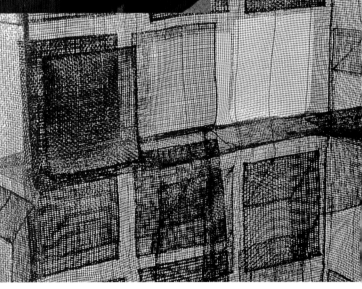

3

Krishna Patel
UNITED STATES

Prarthna Ni Yaadi

Handwoven, double weave, shibori, fulled, discharged, dyed; wool, linen, cotton, silk; each 33 to 46 in long, 12 to 18 in. wide. Photo: Mike Lundgren

This is part of my "Memory of My Prayer Series." In my work, I explore my experience of prayer and meditation as a process for achieving inner calm and peace.

4

Jiseon Lee
UNITED STATES

Buildings: Reflections

Hand and machine stitched, pieced; plastic screen, cotton, nylon, yarn; each section 48 by 48 in. Photo: Colorado State University

My works are inspired by urban architectural spaces, layers, and transparency.

3

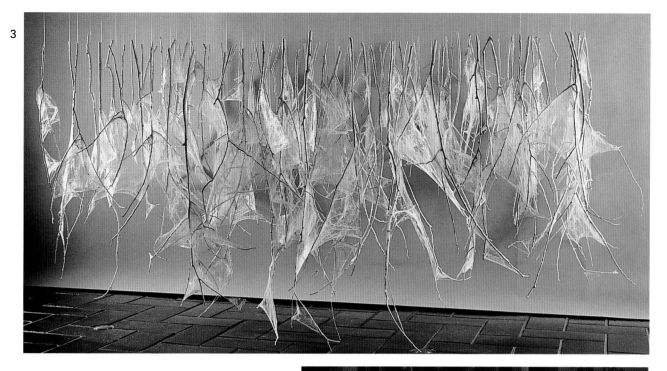

1

Mary Babcock
UNITED STATES

In Praise of Nymphs at Tybee

Hand stitched, appliquéd, embroidered, constructed; silk, steel, sea items, oleander and palm leaves; 13 by 12 by 12 ft.

2

Katharine Cobey
UNITED STATES

Boat with Four Figures

Hand carved, spun, knitted; wool, spruce, stainless steel, plastic fishing line; 6 by 30 by 14 ft. Photo: David Boyce Cobey

3

Yoko Kataoka
JAPAN

Yellow Illusion

Constructed, painted; zelkova tree branches, floss, silk, acrylic paint; 48 by 72 by 36 in.

I'm charmed by any kind of nest—bird's nest, spider's web, bee hive, and so on. I'm trying to make them too.

4

Jayson K. Taylor
UNITED STATES

Waiting for Blue

Fused fabric, video projected; silk organza, satin, mattress ticking, batting, video equipment; 6 by 10 by 4 ft.

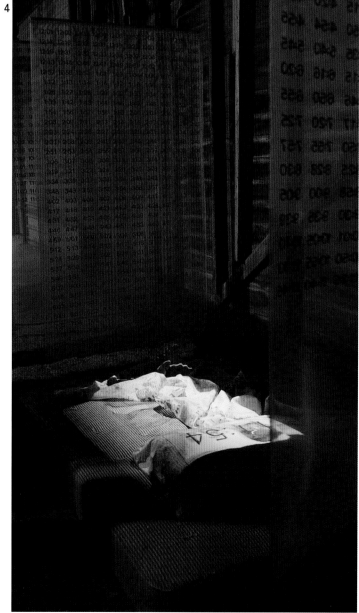

1

2

3

[image of textile columns installation]

4

1
Zane Berzina
ENGLAND

Tattoos

Hand woven, ikat painted, transfer and screen printed; polyester, cotton, metallic fabric; each piece 100 by 39 in. Photo: Laimonis Stipnieks

This installation is a mixed-media textiles prototype collection inspired by Pacific designs and body ornamentations. It is a translation of the simplicity of Pacific design to Western tastes. It is a complex of vividly colored, sculpturally woven, and primitively printed textiles.

2
Marie-Laure Ilie
UNITED STATES

Alter Egos

Heat transfer, painted, assembled; silk organza, plastic, cellophane, stones; 84 by 48 by 48 in.

3
Cas Holmes
ENGLAND

Columns

Layered, dyed, stitched, glued; paper, thread, wood, dye; 4 to 7 ft. by 1 to 1½ ft. Photo: Enrillo Saccatorre

I like to use discarded items, waste material no longer considered useful. Recycled materials and waste have a history. These I break down, tear, and cut until they are reassembled to create something more meaningful. Fragments and layers mark the passing of time, the rituals of making, acting as part of the narrative of the work.

4
Kyoung Ae Cho
UNITED STATES

Path

Stitched, sliced; wood, fabric, thread; 16 by 264 in. variable.

1

2

3

opposite page

Louise Lemieux Bérubé
CANADA

Silence of Winter

Jacquard, taquet-woven; metallics, silk, polyester; 96 by 54 in. Photo: Michel Dubreuil

Trees have been very present in my artwork since my beginning as a weaver. Their texture, their stability, their strength, their silent presence, and their multiple colors inspire me. I always come back to this soothing vitality.

1

Pauline Verbeek-Cowart
UNITED STATES

Silk Forest

Handwoven jacquard; sized Indian silk, perle cotton; 90 by 29 in.

Working on a jacquard loom allows me to explore the complexity and structural beauty of the woven surface while using materials and processes that are essential to the expression of an image.

2

Martha Fieber
UNITED STATES

Woven Hemlock

Hand woven, dyed, embroidered; rayon ribbon, thread; 8¼ by 4¼ in. Photo: Craig Woerpel

3

Emily K. Robertson
UNITED STATES

Spring Comes to Elm Road

Hooked, dyed; wool; 26½ by 18 in.

1

1

Maya Schonenberger
UNITED STATES

Twilight of the Trees

Thread painted, raw-edge appliquéd and pieced, machine quilted; acrylic and oil paint, canvas, cotton, silk, and wool fabric; 82 by 60 in.
Photo: Gerhard Heidersberger

2

Vita Marie Lovett
UNITED STATES

Primitive Door Series #21: Quail Cottage Barn

Machine thread-painted, machine quilted; canvas, cotton, acrylic paint, thread; 23 by 24 in.
Photo: Bread + Butter Photography

I enjoy the challenge of creating the illusion of rustic wood and peeling paint through fabric and thread.

3

Sally Agee
UNITED STATES

Hooked for Life

Punch hooked; wool yarn, monks cloth; 57 by 46 in.
Photo: John Barber

4

Linda Friedman Schmidt
UNITED STATES

Salsa Cures Sadness

Hooked; recycled clothing, cotton-warp cloth; 60 by 42 in.

Just as the artist transforms old clothes into art, rug hooking into painting, obsessive-woman's work into exhibition-worthy work, these salsa dancers are beginning their own transformation.

5

Amy C. Clarke
UNITED STATES

Dreamer of Dreams

Bead embroidered; Japanese seed beads, cotton canvas, thread; 5¼ by 6½ in.

The dreamer is my nephew caught at a thoughtful moment. He seems wise beyond his 3½ years, and the future seems ripe with potential in his young eyes. As I stitch down the beads, I stitch down the fleeting moments and stories that happen as I'm beading.

6

Patty Yoder
UNITED STATES

Esther

Hooked; wool, cotton; 44 by 30 in.
Photo: John Sherman

Esther was my mentor who made me understand the quest for the perfect piece of wool.

2

3

5

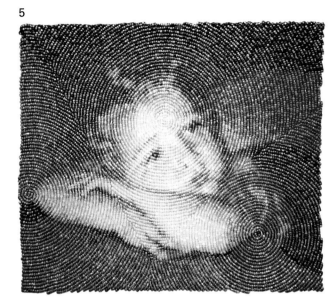

4

6

1

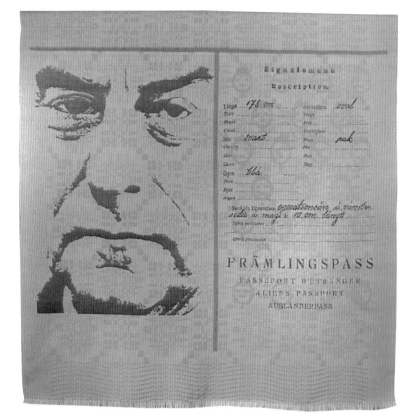

1

Vita Plume
UNITED STATES

Alien's Passport

Jacquard woven; cotton; 55 by 65 in.
Photo: Karen Rouet

I combine images, symbols, patterns, and text from family history and my Latvian cultural background to address issues of displacement, cultural duality, erasure, and loss. This piece interweaves an image of my father and his passport information when he was located in Sweden after the Second World War.

2

Frances Dorsey
CANADA

Four Squares

Jacquard woven, two wefts; linen, cotton; 40 by 40 in.
Photo: Steve Farmer

In common with many of my generation, I grew up with a father who relived his World War II combat experiences daily. In my work, the war becomes an analogy for whatever swords our lives cough up before us. We all have our own melting points, but refining fire for our souls nonetheless.

4

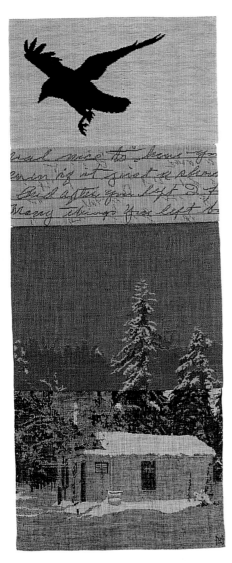

6

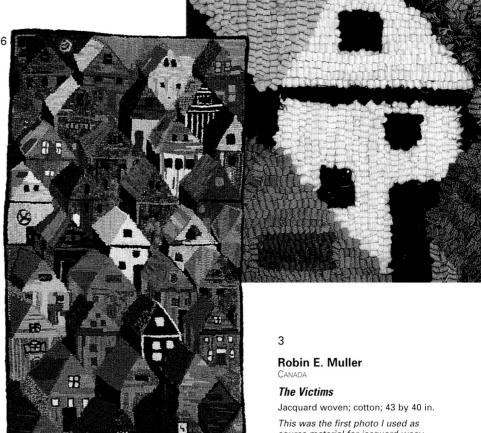

3

Robin E. Muller
CANADA

The Victims

Jacquard woven; cotton; 43 by 40 in.

This was the first photo I used as source material for jacquard weaving. The image is directly from an Ottawa newspaper. I identified with these passive victims of September 11. We were people of different color, united in the horror of what we had seen. We would return to our families that night, but we were changed forever.

4

Marie Westerman
UNITED STATES

Things You Left Behind

Woven, pick-up double- and triple-weave, sewn; linen thread; 39 by 15½ in. Photo: Peter Lee

5

Trish Johnson
CANADA

Machias Seal Island

Hooked, dyed, overdyed; wool, linen; 27 by 37 in. Photo: Joseph Bengel

6

Olga Rothschild
UNITED STATES

Suburban Geometric

Hooked; wool strips, linen; 47 by 27 in. Photo: David Bitters

1

2

3

3

4

6

5

5
Sheila O'Hara
<small>United States</small>

Blossom Creek
Jacquard loom-woven; cotton yarn;
19 by 25 in.

6
Roslyn Logsdon
<small>United States</small>

Montmajour
Hooked; wool, linen; 29s½ by 20 in.
Photo: Linda Zandler

1

1

Sharmini Wirasekara
CANADA

Sea of Life Kimono

Peyote off-loom woven; Japanese glass beads, metallic-silk fabric, plastic stand; 9 by 6½ by 1 in. Photo: Barbara Cohen.

In designing this kimono, I used traditional Asian symbols to emphasize different aspects of life. Waves represent the sea and water; goldfish stand for happiness; lotus is the Buddhist symbol of purity and also symbolizes nature; mountains depict earth and long life; clouds and sun are for heaven.

2

Jette Nevers
DENMARK

Rubber Tops

Woven; polyester-coated polyurethane; 8 by 2½ ft. Photo: Ole Akhøj

3

Andrea Berez
UNITED STATES

A Little Mental Yoga

Woven, quad-weave; rayon, cotton; 19 by 59 in. Photo: Maureen Monte

Quad-weave is a four-layer, double-weave pickup technique in which all four layers are woven simultaneously on the loom.

2

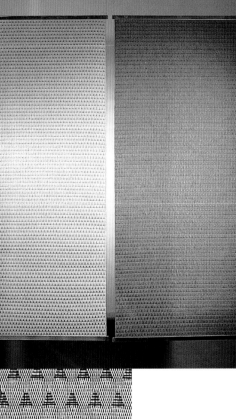

3

4

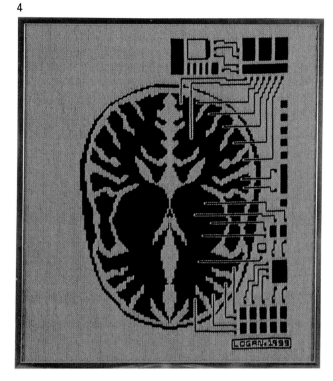

5

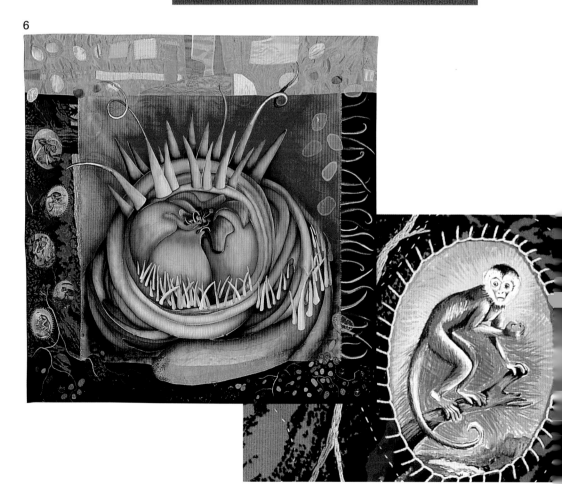

6

4
W. Logan Fry
United States

Digital Interface

Finnwoven, paired double-weave pick-up; wool; 19 by 17 in. Photo: Heather Protz. Collection of The Minneapolis Institute of Arts

The brain is woven with the traces of our sensations, the relics of our memories, now augmented with information technology and the digital interface.

5
Jaye Campbell
United States

Summer and Winter
(Reversible altar cloth and veil)

Shown here: Summer

Handwoven, soumak inlay, embroidered; linen, ramie, silk; altar cloth 35 by 30 in., veil 24 by 24 in. Photo: Brian McLernon

6
Kathy Weaver
United States

Growth: Nano Version

Airbrushed, appliquéd, embroidered, painted, embellished; satin, velvet, glass, pebbles, egg tempera; 64 by 51 in.

My work consists of microscopic, organic forms enhanced with hand embroidery and painted vignettes. Details are shown on a macro scale, inviting the viewer to be like an emotive nanorobot exploring an alien environment.

1

2

3

1

Bette Uscott-Woolsey
UNITED STATES

Surface Texture II

Dyed, embroidered, painted, machine pieced; silk, embroidery thread, fabric and airbrush paint; 31 by 23 in. Photo: Will Brown

2

Linda Levin
UNITED STATES

10048 II

Dyed, machine stitched; cotton; 54 by 42 in. Photo: Image Inn

This is based on 9/11—trying to capture the mood of that time— nothing literal.

3

Kathyanne White
UNITED STATES

Illusion

Hand dyed, pieced, sewn; cotton, dye, canvas; 72 by 45 in.

4

Cathy Bolding
UNITED STATES

Spiral Aloe

Jacquard woven; cotton, linen, polyester, metallic thread; 37 by 34 in.

I consider myself both a weaver and a photographer. Lately, I have been spending many wonderful hours at the University of California Botanical Garden.

5

Fuyuko Matsubara
UNITED STATES

In the Earth: Part XI

Woven, painted warp and weft; hand-plied linen, cotton, silk, and rayon yarn; 32 by 42 in.

1

Nelda Warkentin
UNITED STATES

Costa Careyes #2

Painted, fused, machine stitched; transparent silk, acrylic paint, fabric, canvas; 42 by 68 in. Photo: John Tuckey

2

Morgan Clifford
UNITED STATES

Sources

Lampas woven, brocade, painted warp; silk, linen; 30 by 64 in. Photo: Peter Lee

When I designed this piece I had just come back from living in Scotland for a few months, and the piece ended up being a kind of collaboration of shapes from my kindergarten roots—circle, square, and triangle—combined with the timelessness of a woven-grid pattern, inspired by a Scottish tartan.

3

3

Michael F. Rohde
UNITED STATES

Spring/Ginza

Block woven with tapestry inlay;
hand-dyed wool, linen; 57 by 48 in.
Photo: Andrew Neuhart

*This series began with the obvious
idea of kimonos, places I had visited
in Japan, and references to place, to
season, and to objects.*

4

Michael James
UNITED STATES

Memento Vivere

Hand painted, digitally developed,
digitally printed; cotton; 57 by 90 in.
Photo: John Nollendorfs

*The OED explains memento vivere
as "a reminder of life; a reminder of
the pleasure of living." It translates
from the Latin as "remember that
you have to live." It seems an appropriate sentiment in a post-apocalyp-
tic age. This fabric construction is a
meditation on life and death. Green
traditionally symbolizes life and
hope, but the pronounced visual textures of the digitally and hand-paint-
ed fabrics also allude to decomposi-
tion, the passing of matter from one
state to another. Nothing is static
within the geometric structure of this
surface; the life force suggested here
is active and transformational.*

4

1

Hye Shin
UNITED STATES

Image III

Woven; linen, hemp, paint;
12 by 12 in.

Inspiration comes from spacious land, sky, and the marvelous scenes of nature. Colors, textures, and structure of textiles have been expressed to visualize a sense of place, space, and time of nature.

2

Martha Warshaw
UNITED STATES

Cope: Burning

Machine pieced, hand tied, bleached; cotton and cotton-blend fabric, bleach; 53 by 106 in.

2

3a

3b

Jennifer Moore
UNITED STATES

We All Look Up

Woven, double-weave pick-up; hand-dyed silk, cotton; 68 by 32 in.
Photo: Hawthorne Studios

4

Blythe Church
CANADA

Cotton Candy

Dyed, woven; cotton, merino wool; 98 by 29 in.

4

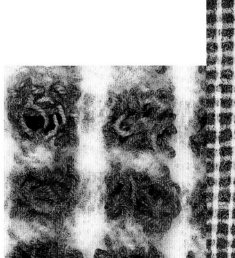

145

1
Betty McMullen
UNITED STATES

...to the Other Side

Woven, painted, appliquéd, fused; cotton warp, commercial fabric, dye, print paste; 42 by 36 in. Photo: Rick Lee

2
Margie Garratt
SOUTH AFRICA

Alpha and Omega

Dyed, machine pieced, machine and hand sewn; cotton, dye, commercial fabric, silk, rayon African fabric; 52¼ by 56½ in.

Inspired by the early-dawn view over part of the Cape Peninsular. I ponder the meaning of life through the metaphor of dawn and dusk.

3
Kristin Rohr
CANADA

Untitled

Dye painted, printed, appliquéd, stitched; linen, silk organza, thread, paint; 9 by 12 in.

4

4

Carol Taylor
UNITED STATES

Too Tall for the Shelf

Hand dyed, hand painted, pieced,
fused, couched, appliquéd, free-
motion stitched; cotton; 83 by 63 in.

*Inspired by the song "Grandfather's
Clock" by Henry Clay Work. "My
Grandfather's clock was too tall for
the shelf/So it stood 90 years on the
floor. It was taller by half than the
old man himself/And it weighed not
a pennyweight more. It was bought
in the morn of the day he was
born/And was always his treasure
and pride. But it stopped—short!—
never to go again/When the old
man died!"*

5

Carol Westfall
UNITED STATES

Anthrax

Computerized, jacquard woven; cotton
warp, glow-in-the-dark-synthetic weft;
46¼ by 14 in. Photo: D. James Dee

*This is part of a trilogy—AIDS, Anthrax,
and Pox. Deadly organisms which are,
in terms of form, texture, and color,
quite magnificent images.*

5

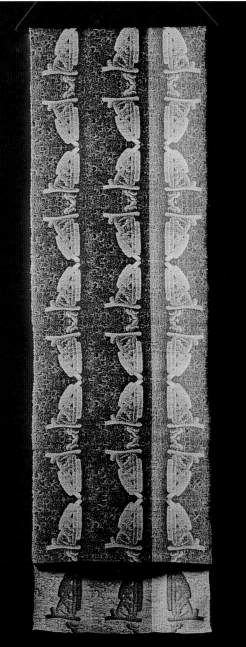

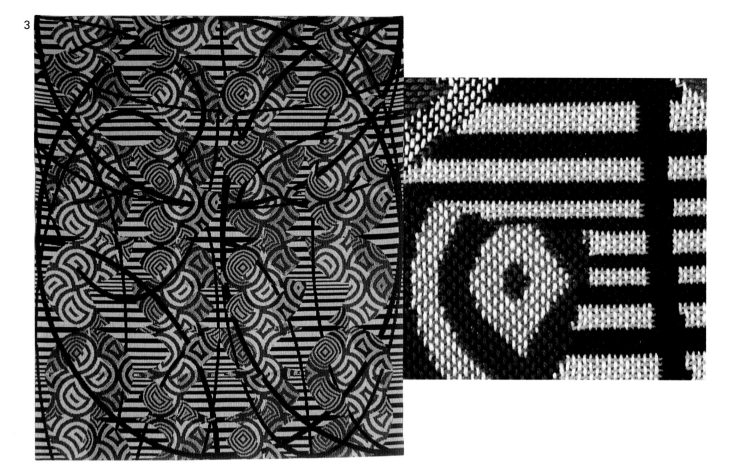

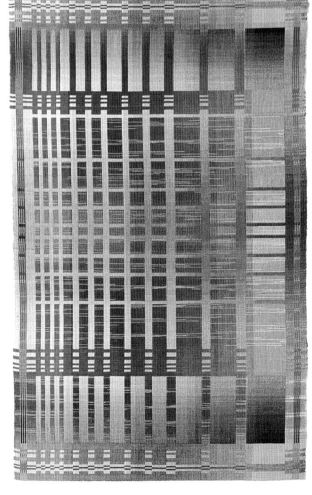

1

Sondra Dorn
United States

Grip

Dyed, pieced, painted, machine and hand embroidered; linen, fiber-reactive dye, thread, textile paint; 21½ by 24 in. Photo: Tim Barnwell

2

Connie Lippert
United States

Take me There

Navajo wedge-weave; naturally dyed wool and linen; 24 by 47 in. Photo: Robert Lippert

Wedge weave is a Navaho weave originating about 1870 to 1890. It is woven diagonally to the lines of the loom, forcing the warp out of the vertical which causes the edges to scallop. This trait, which I find exciting, is the reason that the Navajo didn't practice it longer. Traders and tourists refused to buy it because of its misshapen appearance.

3

Janice Lessman-Moss
United States

Turn the Clock to Zero #2

Jacquard woven, triple weave; cotton; 56 by 49 in.

4

Nancy Middlebrook
United States

Grey Ikat #6

Woven, double-weave, ikat; hand-dyed yarn; 28 by 18 in. Photo: Paul Joslin

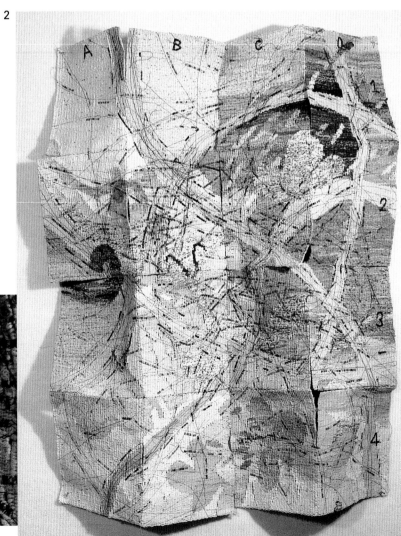

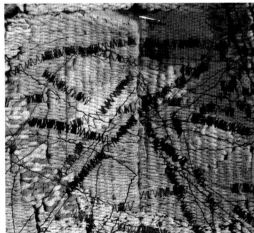

3

1

George-Ann Bowers
UNITED STATES

Little House in the Big Woods

Woven, double-weave pick-up, painted, stitched; cotton, linen, and silk thread, textile paint, cotton; 45 by 45 in. Photo: Dana Davis Photography

This piece is a non-quilt. It was woven on a floor loom in a single piece in the pattern of a quilt. The woven pattern is comprised of four log-cabin blocks, each spiraling around its own central red-hearth square which was painted on the warp and woven with a red weft.

2

Si-Yun Chang
UNITED STATES

My Journey

Woven, machine embroidered; paper thread, sewing thread; 43 by 32½ in.

3

Irina Kolesnikova
RUSSIA

Transition

Woven; flax, silk, 15 by 11 in.

4

Feliksas Jakubauskas
LITHUANIA

Reflections in the Wind

Woven; wool, silk, synthetic fiber; 51 by 74 in.

4

1

Sarah Mays-Salin
United States

Ya Bari I

Jacquard woven, appliquéd, dip
dyed, cotton warp, silk and rayon
weft; 32 by 25 in.
Photo: George Post

*Inspired by the visual and life-cycle
patterning of butterfly wings, my
work has explored associated con-
cepts of transformation, death, and
renewal. My process, too, has
become metaphoric—the binding and
unbinding of threads for resist dyeing
recalls the forming and breaking of
the chrysalis.*

2

Liz Alpert Fay
United States

Wheels of Fortune

Hand dyed, hooked, braided; recycled
and commercial wool, burlap, dye; 27
by 42 in. Photo: Brad Stanton

3

3

Anne McKenzie Nickolson
United States

Off the Edge

Hand appliquéd, machine pieced;
cotton broadcloth; 57½ by 68¼ in.

4

Kris Johnson
United States

Progression

Woven; cotton warp, monofili-
ment weft; 48 by 96 in. Photo:
Michele Dion

4

wearables

2

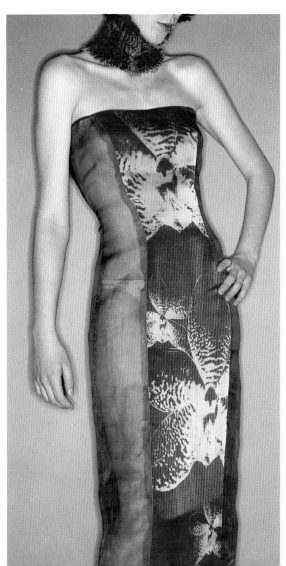

opposite page

**Grethe Wittrock
and Ann Schmidt-
Christensen**
DENMARK

**The Horse (from the Jeune
Couture Collection)**

Handwoven plain weave, screen
printed; Japanese-paper yarn, viscose. Photo: Jeppe Gudmundsen-
Holmgreen

*Project PaperMoon is our experi-
ment with vegetable Japanese-
paper yarns and paper sheets, modi-
fied into textiles and formed as func-
tional sculptural clothing.*

1

Karren K. Brito
UNITED STATES

Dry Savannah Pelt (two views)

White-shadow and arashi shibori;
silk, glass beads, metal logo. Photo:
Joe Van De Hatert

*My goal is to combine color and tex-
ture in such a way that the texture
makes the color shimmer, and the
color accentuates the texture.*

2

Heather Nania
UNITED STATES

Orchid Dress

Screen printed, discharged, shibori
heat-set; silk organza, charmeuse.
Photo: M Studios

1

Cheri Reckers
UNITED STATES

Peacock Ensemble

Dyed, hand painted, hand and machine stitched; silk/rayon/stretch velvet, silk satin georgette, silk double-crepe georgette, feathers, dyes, gutta resist.
Photo: Michael Ceschiat

Inspired by neighboring peacocks whose quiet elegance unfolds into a dramatic display with a profusion of color.

2

Kayla Kennington
UNITED STATES

Fire Blossom Phoenix

Quilted, digitized, embroidered, draped, pin-tucked; Vietnamese silk, Cambodian organza, beads, thread.
Photo: Perrault Studios

This piece was done as a tribute to the villagers in Vietnam who create this wonderful fabric. It won the "Crème de la Crème" top award for the Bernina Fashion Show in 2002.

3

Koos Van Den Akker
UNITED STATES

Circles Swing Coat

Appliquéd, taped, couched, quilted; cashmere, rayon, silk taffeta, wool yarn, flocked chiffon. Photo: Larry Friar

2

3

4

5

6

4

Kay Disbrow
UNITED STATES

Tibetan Prayer Bead

Dye painted, dextrin resist, sewn; silk/rayon velvet. Photo: Peter Kricker (Emily Barzin, model)

These pieces were created as a personal resistance to violence in our culture, using a touchstone—a Tibetan prayer bead—as a reminder of the many traditions of work toward inner peace.

5

Satu Itäpää
FINLAND

Wasps' Nest Dress and Honeycomb Scarf

Free-motion machine embroidered, dyed; vegetable dye, silk thread, water soluble stabilizer.

6

Cynthia McGuirl
UNITED STATES

Kimono 74

Woven, sewn; cotton warp, rayon chenille weft.

My current weaving uses rayon chenille on a fine cotton warp in polychrome summer and winter weave. This combination creates a visual language of rug design in a soft, velvety fabric that is brought to life by the wearer.

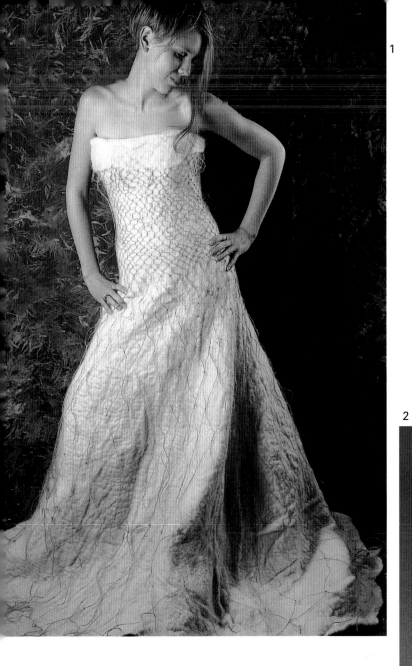

Thomas Horst
UNITED STATES

Entrapment

Felted, knotted; wool, twine.
Photo: Ken Love

2

Peter Ciesla
UNITED STATES

Mother-of-Pearl

Bead embroidered, sewn; buttons,
glass beads, wool, cotton, linen, silk,
polyester netting.

2

3

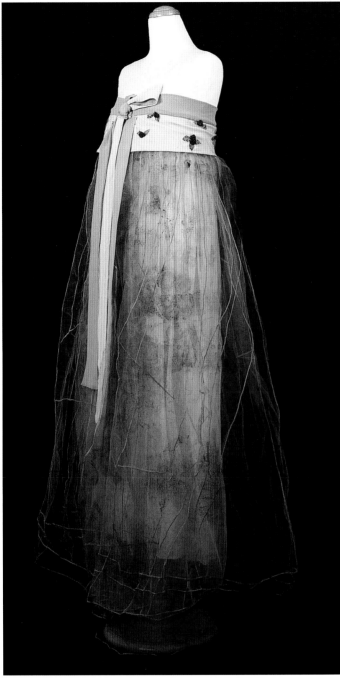

3

Jiwoon Kim
CANADA

Spring

Dyed, sewn, screen printed, woven, embroidered; polyester, silk, cotton, polyester net.

4

Leea Pienimäki
FINLAND

I am; I think

Sculpted, sewn; metal web, tulle, nylon monofilament.

This piece depicts human existence and the vanishing nature of a woman's dreams; the frail border zone or transition between consciousness and the unconscious; the disappearing of gravity, substance becoming unsubstantial, mental.

4

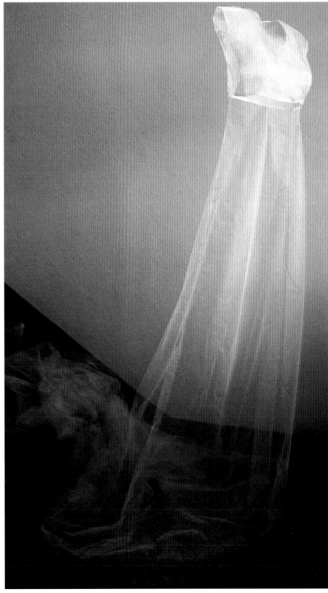

1

Vishna Collins
AUSTRALIA

Masquerade

Split, rolled, knotted, crocheted; raffia, satin ribbon, lace. Photo: John Cleasby

2

Nikki Willis
ENGLAND

Fake

Hand felted and embroidered; linen, wool tops, embroidery thread.
Photo: Michael Wicks

This work was made for an exhibition at the Victoria and Albert Museum in London. The work was inspired by a nightgown that belonged to Thomas Coutts. The original garment was a reproduction ermine.

4

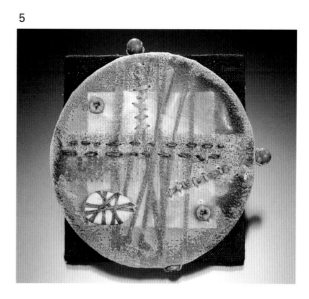

5

6

3

Christine Culver
UNITED STATES

Harlequin Dress

Stitched; recycled plastic-mesh fruit and vegetable bags, monofilament thread. Photo: Kate Cameron

Plastic mesh is very forgiving. The perceived delicacy of the designs are ironically brought to life by the durable, disposable plastic mesh used for packaging. I call it ironic couture.

4

Chris Tait
and Kirstie LeQuesne
NEW ZEALAND

Connection and Protection Cloak

Machine pieced and quilted, dyed, hand and machine appliquéd, woven, braided; cotton, beads, feathers; 46½ by 28 in. Photo: Neil MacBeth

A collaboration between mother and daughter, this cloak expresses our connection to each other, our shared and individual heritage, and our connection to Aotearoa, New Zealand.

5

Kara Tennis
UNITED STATES

Brooch: Over Time

Hand stitched; silk, silk chiffon, hand-made paper, paper yarn, beeswax, found objects, nylon thread; 2 by 2¼ in. Photo: Ralph Gabriner

Influx from the spiritual world fills the vessels we become, shaped by the ineffable beauty of the world around us and the choices we make each moment.

6

Kathy Bunce
UNITED STATES

Shoulder bag

Loom woven, sewn; Japanese beads, satin, thread; 7⅝ by 16¼ in. Photo: Jack Toolin

1

Eva S. Walsh
UNITED STATES

I am the Day; I am the Night

Beaded, embellished, embroidered, fringed; seed beads, pearls, crystals; 28 by 6 in. Photo: Randall Smith

My signature is the mirror image of the design in the fringe.

2

Kay Dolezal
UNITED STATES

Collar and Container

Right-angle weave stitched; glass beads, wood armature; collar 15 by 15 in., box 6 by 6 in. Photo: Steve Gyurina

When not being worn, the collar can be folded and stored in the low box. Or, the collar can be spread on a horizontal surface with the box turned over and placed in the center.

3

Rachel Starr Suntop
UNITED STATES

Anemone Hat

Sewn, glued, knitted; silk, pine needles, yarn, wax, wire; 12 by 18 by 18 in. Photo: Larry Gawel

4

Camille Lord
AUSTRALIA

The Chrysler Building: Blue

Scanned, digitized, machine embroidered; drawings, rayon, cotton, and invisible thread, silk, plastic handle segments; 10 by 6 in.

Whimsical response to the glorious Bakelite handle. The Art Deco shape of each segment needed to be interpreted in waves of blue light.

5

Robin L. Bergman
UNITED STATES

Beaded Headpiece

Off-loom beaded, square-stitch crocheted; Japanese and Czech seed beads, thread; 6½ by 14 in. diameter. Photo: Gordon S. Bernstein

3

4

5

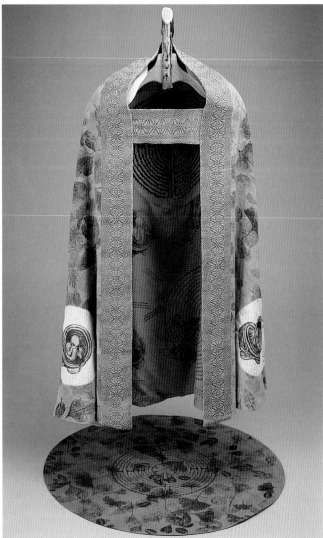

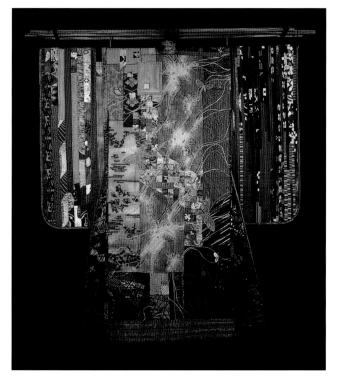

1

Sheila Niles
CANADA

***My Mother Always Wanted to
Go to Japan (front and back with
detail of front)***

Strip and paper pieced, couched,
dyed, sashiko and shibori reverse
appliquéd, hand and machine
stitched; fabric, dye.

*The cross-stitch panels were done
by my mother 60 years ago for an
altar frontal. They came into my
hands just as I had completed the
kimono and have eerily provided the
finishing touch to this memorial.*

3

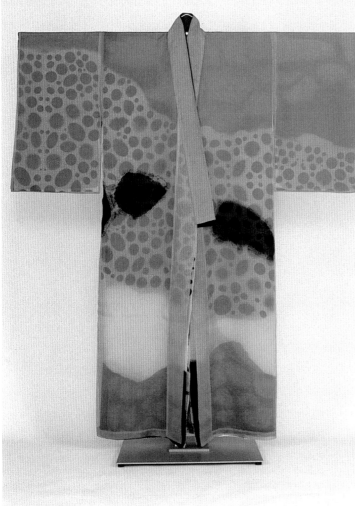

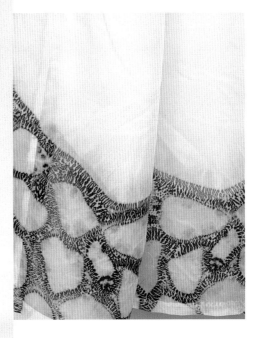

2

Ruth Seider
UNITED STATES

4

Sacred Path I: Psalm 23:4

Dyed, woven, screen printed, painted, free-motion machine embroidered; linen, silk, rayon yarn, canvas, dye, pigment. Photo: Bill Lemke

This is an exploration of the path we walk toward the sacred, based on the Medieval cope, a religious garment. All of my work contains the image of the labyrinth—a metaphor for this walk.

3

Barbara Rogers
AUSTRALIA

Healing Waters

Shibori, discharged, azolc dyed; silk organza. Photo: Warwick Clarke

4

Ann Clarke
UNITED STATES

Universal Balance

Machine knitted, fulled, needlepoint; wool, floss; 52 by 56 in.

5

1

Yvonne Wakabayashi
CANADA

Deep Waters

Arashi shibori, discharge printed, metallic screen printed; silk organza, gunma silk. Photo: Dianella Knight

2

June Gaddy
UNITED STATES

Migration: Harlem

Screen printed, beaded, sewn; silk, cotton, beads, dress form, suitcase.

Inspired by the migration of African-Americans from the rural south to the urban north.

3

Verônica Franca
SWEDEN

Nosferatu

Stitched; rubber strings.
Photo: Leslie Lesley Spinks

6

7

4

Lizabeth Shannon
UNITED STATES

Cecropia Shawl

Woven, yarn dyed with bound resists, fulled; organic cotton, merino wool, indigo, madder, and iron dye; 32 by 60 in. Photo: Steve Mann

Using natural fibers and dyes, my handwoven fabrics reflect nature while connecting me to the earth.

5

Christine Keller
GERMANY

Scarves: Contrast

Hand woven, felted; merino wool, mercerized cotton; 9 by 66 in. Photo: Cornelia Feyll

These scarves are part of a series designed with Anna Biro of Montreal, Canada for the German company, Handweberei im Rosenwinkel, where they are produced and marketed.

6

Kay Faulkner
AUSTRALIA

Coral Polyps

Hand woven, dyed, loom-controlled shibori, supplementary warps; cotton/acrylic, wool; 32 by 80 in. Photo: Andrea Higgins

Inspired by the coral formations of the Great Barrier Reef. The living reef is made up of millions of tiny coral polyps.

7

Shelly DeChantal
UNITED STATES

Aspen Devoré Scarf

Bomaki shibori, devoré, painted, discharged, printed; silk/rayon scarf, dye, discharge, etching medium; 12 by 60 in. Photo: John Bonath

1

3

2

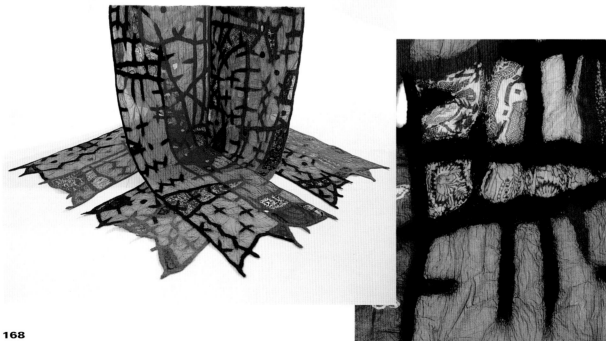

4

Skye and Peter Ciesla
UNITED STATES

The Venetian

Constructed, embroidered; wool, wire, thread, aquamarine chips, glass beads.

3

Sarah F. Saulson
UNITED STATES

Checkmate Scarf

Hand woven, painted warp, hand-plied fringe; silk, cotton, rayon; 9 by 72 in. Photo: David W. Coulter

1

Lindy Chinnery
NEW ZEALAND

Rajasthani Wrap

Woven, plain-collapsed weave, warp dyed; mohair, merino wool, silk, acrylic, stretch wool, beads; 24 by 75 in. Photo: Elizabeth Goodal

2

Jorie Johnson
JAPAN

Pomegranate and Green Plum

Hand felted; Indian cotton, wool; each 17 by 120 in. Photo: Y. Kobayashi

From the "Stained-glass Shawl" series, this work was juried first-prize winner in the "New Wave: New Fibres-New Techniques" exhibition at Convergence 2002, Vancouver, Canada. Expression based on utilizing leftover scraps of fabric by binding them together during the felting process as opposed to construction by needle and thread.

5

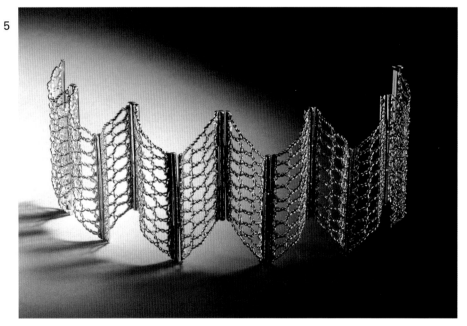

5

Hanne E. Behrens
DENMARK

Untitled Bracelet

Metal lacework; silver, gold; 7 by 2 in. Photo: Ole Akhoj

6

Bice D'Errico
ITALY

Blue Drop

Crocheted; gold wire, opal, pearls; 16 by 3⅛ in. Photo: Aleph-Como

6

4

5

1

Joyce Kliman
UNITED STATES

Japanese Images

Discharged, overdyed, stamped,
photo transfered, patchworked,
embroidered; cotton, linen.
Photo: Bob Barrett

2

Phyllis Christenson
UNITED STATES

Moonlight Shadows

Machine pieced, quilted, hand sewn;
Thai and Japanese silk, Chinese jade
carvings. Photo: Pat Pollard

*I view each of my garments as a
work of haiku—the painterly love of
the visual, layers of illusion, sponta-
neous feeling, hidden treasures and
meaning, sharing of the spirit in
hopes of touching another.*

3

Anita Luvera Mayer
UNITED STATES

Rags to Riches

Woven, dyed, machine embroidered;
silk, rayon. Photo: Roger Schreiber.
(Zenn Jones, model)

4

Alexis Abrams
UNITED STATES

Gray and Gold Coat

Hand painted, block printed, pieced,
sewn; silk crepe, dye.
Photo: Barry Abrams

5

Jane Herzenberg
UNITED STATES

Lyrical Kimono: Volcano

Hand painted, devoré; satin, silk.
Photo: R. Toby

1

Deborah Hird Newell
UNITED STATES

New Block: Fringed Coat and Shawl

Hand woven, hand painted; custom-spun rayon bouclé, textile paint, templates. Photo: John Cooper. (Peter Brown, stylist)

Currently, I am playing with the juxtaposition of organic and geometric shapes and find constant delight in the subtleties and variations intrinsic in my process.

2

Doshi
UNITED STATES

Red Tempest

Shibori, discharged, dyed; silk organza. Photo: Tom Henderson

In my work, the soft edges, shapes, and shadows left in the fabric, the colors that resonate with life's richness, the textures that reflect dynamism and sensuality, all create dynamic, graceful, and evocative statements.

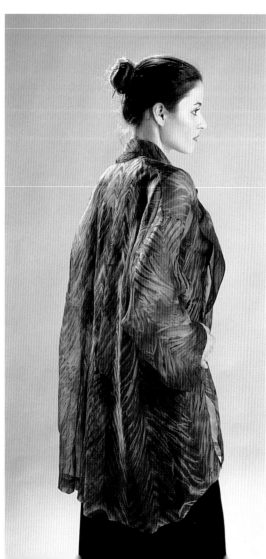

3

Sandra Clark
UNITED STATES

Inside/Out Coat

Hand painted, pieced, machine embellished, burnout; silk, velvet, linen canvas, suede. Photo: Bob Barrett

4

Suzanne Perilman
UNITED STATES

Bamboo Jacket over Fan Shirt

Discharged, over printed, sewn; black organza, metallic pigments, hand-cut paper stencils. Photo: Pat Pollard

5

Erika Mock
UNITED STATES

Day's Eye Sweater

Intarsia knitted; Egyptian cotton. Photo: Jeff Frey

6

Fern Wayne
UNITED STATES

Coat, Scarf, Pocketbook #1

Hand loomed, double knit; rayon chenille and wool yarn, vintage buttons. Photo: Joe Bowman

5

4

6

1

1

Carol Kurtz
UNITED STATES

Marble Shibori Jacket

Machine knitted, felted, marble shibori; merino wool.

The human and organic nature of felted-shibori clothing make for wearable human sculpture.

2

Iwona Rypesc-Kostovic
UNITED STATES

Foggy Morning

Hand dyed, hand and machine loomed, collaged, hand tailored; silk and rayon, textured-metallic and rayon thread.
Photo: Cedomir Kostovic

3

Anna Carlson
UNITED STATES

Autumn Swing Jacket

Stitched, couched, appliquéd, shrunk; hand-dyed cotton velveteen, thread. Photo: Cheryl Walsh Bellville

In my recent work, I create a textured fabric with stitching and shrinking. Then additional stitching, machine embroidery, painting and appliqué are used to create a pattern on the surface.

4

Carol Lee Shanks and Kathryn Alexander
UNITED STATES

Sedimentary Stripe Tunic

Hand spun, dyed, woven, pieced, pleated; cashmere, silk, rayon, merino wool. Photo: Jacinta Bouwkamp

3

2

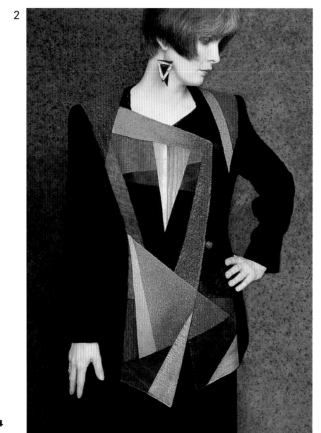

4

5

6

5

Nika Feldman
UNITED STATES

Where Has She Been, II
Dyed, screen printed, devoré, hand stitched, constructed; cotton muslin, thread.
Photo: Nika Feldman

6

Pia Filliger-Nolte
GERMANY

Overall and Dress
Ondulée woven; silk, cotton.
Photo: Georg Jahnke

diversions

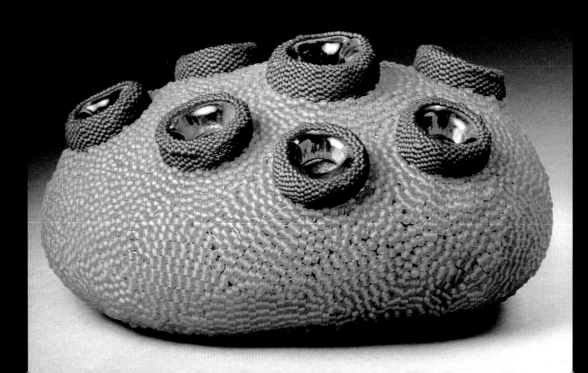

1

2

3

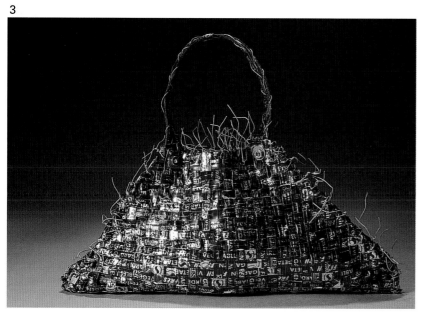

opposite page
Chris Allen-Wickler
UNITED STATES

Green Fuse

Peyote stitch; beads, thread, antique glass, stone; 6 by 10 by 5 in. Photo: Peter Lee

1
Christine Culver
UNITED STATES

Sushi Bowl

Felted, dyed, stitched; wool, dye, thread; 5 by 10 in. diameter. Photo: Kate Cameron

2
Charlotte A. LaRoy
UNITED STATES

Jump Rope Basket

Random woven; reed, commercial jump ropes; 9 by 15 by 14 in. Photo: Dave Russell

I maintain one can weave baskets with non-traditional materials. I love the bright, cheerful effect of this basket.

3
Margaret Starrett
UNITED STATES

A Tisket a Tasket

Woven; grocery-store ties, phone wire, washers; 10 by 12 by 3½ in. Photo: Gugger Petter

A fun piece!

1

Katharine Cobey
UNITED STATES

Throw Caution to the Winds II

Diagonally knitted; plastic tape; 7¾ by 2 ft. Photo: David B. Cobey

Knitting can be seriously funny.

2

Loren Schwerd
UNITED STATES

The Accordionist

Sewn; canvas, steel stand; 67 by 24 in.

This work is a video created with choreographer Martha Brim. It was one in a series of short performances that were linked by the motifs of breath, power, and struggle. They were performed at the Columbia Museum of Art in South Carolina. "The Accordionist" was performed by dancer Sarah Jensen to Breathe, an original composition by Trevor Weton.

3
Mary Hettmansperger
UNITED STATES

"They're Coming to Take Me Away"

Full-twist twined; waxed linen; 16 by 5 in. diameter.
Photo: Jeff Baird

Remember this song? I was always puzzled by the lyrics about bas-ketweavers. There is not one bas-ketweaver I know who would sit and twiddle their thumbs and toes. They would be weaving!

4
Clare Qualmann
ENGLAND

Knitted Cover for 3 Kids

Hand knitted; mohair wool; largest child 4 ft. 8 in.; smallest 3 ft. 6 in.

This piece was inspired by a spate of news about child-safety debates over whether children should be allowed to walk to school alone or to play outside. I thought that if you put them in one of these they'd be safely protected from the world, and very warm.

5
Ruth Tabancay
UNITED STATES

Sweet Dreams

Hand stitched, tied; teabags, embroi-dery floss, muslin, batting, card-board base; 40 by 66 in. Photo: Scott Braley

As I helped my daughter with her geometry homework, we sat on her bed, snuggling in her comforter and drinking cups of herbal tea. Those teabags and those special moments inspired this piece.

4
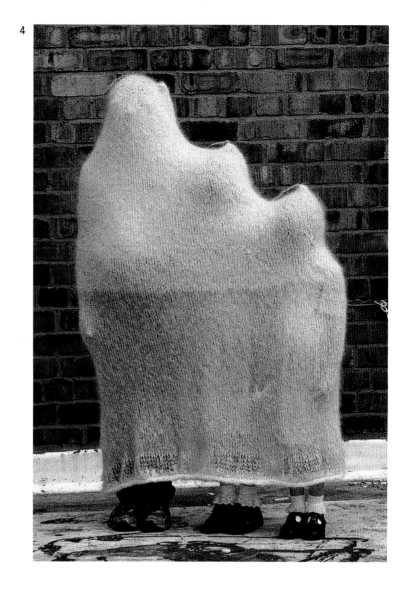

5

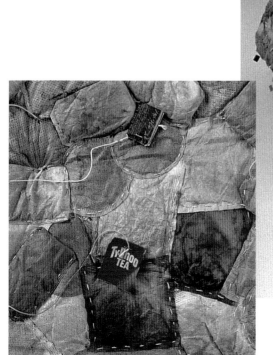

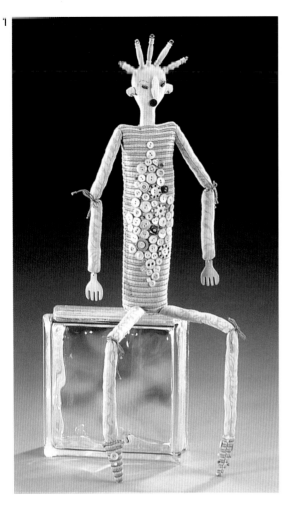

1

Deble Faulkner
UNITED STATES

Button Collector

Sewn; fiber, buttons, beads; 23 by 7
by 7 in. Photo: Hap Sakwa

2

JoAnn Baumann
UNITED STATES

Memories of Mexico

Bead embroidered, off-loom woven,
fringed; seed beads, antique
sequins, embellishment beads, fabric, fiberfill; 7 by 5 by 2 in. Photo:
Tom Van Eynde

*Vivid color, lush dense foliage, won-
derful costumes, and spectacular
underwater sights all combined to
inspire this fanciful, embroidered
piece.*

3

Ann Citron
UNITED STATES

Agile Dancer

Wrapped, beaded, sewn; wire, seed
beads, sequins, fabric; 16 by 20 in.
Photo: Alex Pohl

*Dancers, being agile and supple,
defy gravity routinely.*

4

5

6

4

Olga Dvigoubsky Cinnamon
UNITED STATES

Piecing Myself Back Together

Crocheted, beaded; waxed linen, cotton and metallic thread, glass beads, jasper, freshwater pearls, cotton stuffing; 9 by 2 by 3 in. Photo: Jeff Owen

Have you ever felt discombobulated? There seem to be moments when the best we can do is to store our "stuff" and suture pieces of our heart, soul, and mind back together.

5

Rosita Johanson
CANADA

A Teapot of Her Own

Hand and machine embroidered; balsa wood, velvet, beads, gold pins, ribbon, metallic thread, paint; 9½ by 7 by 5½ in. Photo: Lenscape Incorporated. Courtesy of Mobilia Gallery, Cambridge, Massachusetts

6

Rebecca Lyon
UNITED STATES

Elemental Sign: Water

Dyed, hand sewn, painted, cast, carved; felt, plastic, dye, concrete paint, real-estate-sign frame; 44 by 28 by 5 in. Photo: Tony Clevenger

1

3

2

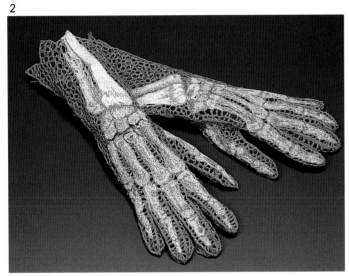

4

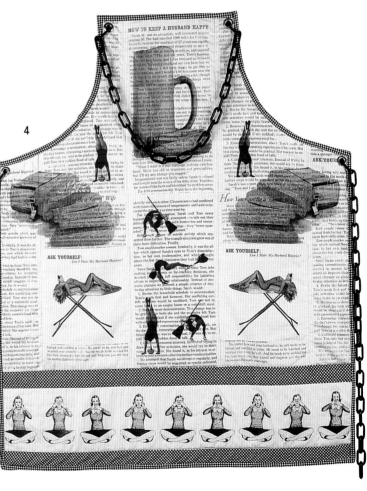

1

Rachel Lawrence Edwards
UNITED STATES

Sole Mates

Beaded, airbrushed, hand stitched, braided, inked, typed; fabric sandals, finishing nails, washers, nuts, glue, beads, metallic yarn, paper, ink, brass; 5 by 10½ in.

2

Kathleen Richert
UNITED STATES

27 Bones

Machine sewn; polyester-cotton thread; each 11 by 3 in.
Photo: Petronella Ytsma

3

David K. Chatt
UNITED STATES

White Men in Suits

Beaded, single-needle right-angle woven; thread, glass seed beads; 6 by 10 by 1¼ in.
Photo: Kozo Takeuchi

Like a crow, I am attracted to things that sparkle. Like a crazy person, I am attracted to the intricate, some would say, obsessive-compulsive nature of beadworking.

4

Cynthia Myerberg
UNITED STATES

How to Keep a Husband Happy

Photo transfer, printed, machine pieced and quilted; cotton, batting, plastic chains; 38 by 30 in.
Photo: M. Gregory Ellis

This apron quilt is from the "Kitschen Help" series. It looks at the propaganda campaigns constructed by the male-dominated mass media following World War II.

5

7

6

5

Franziska Kurth
Denmark

In the Morning When I Rise

Kilim and Gobelin tapestry; silk, wool, cotton; 15¾ by 19¾ in.

In the morning when we rise, we often can't see very clearly, and sometimes you see something out of your last dreams or wishes. You are still in another world and coming step-by-step down to reality.

6

Lynn Mayne
United States

Allergy Sufferers

Tapestry; wool, cotton; 22 by 62 in.

I enjoyed playing with some of Picasso's images of women to deal with my multiple allergies which are under control but still an almost daily annoyance. At least I'm not allergic to wool!

7

Salley Mavor
United States

George's Chair

Embroidered, wrapped; wool felt, upholstery fabric, cardboard, lace, wire, beads, paper; 10 by 10 by 1 in.
Photo: Doug Mindell

1

Susan Shie and James Acord
UNITED STATES

The Cookbook/Hierophant

Airbrushed, painted, hand quilted, embroidered, beaded; cotton, paint, batting, beads, buttons, antique rhinestones; 61 by 71 in. Photo: Brian Blauser, B & B Studios

This is card #5 in our "Kitchen Tarot" series. There are actually two quilts in this piece as one panel is sewn along its top onto the larger panel. The smaller panel is the tarot card, and it can be lifted up to reveal the painting hidden behind it.

2

Christine Ambrose
UNITED STATES

Holy Cow! La Vaca Sagrada de Guadalupe

Hand painted, wax resist, beaded, quilted, embroidered; commercial fabric, silk jacquard, dye, beads, cotton, rayon, silk, and metallic thread, batting; 26 by 13½ in. Photo: Carol Krueger

3

Marilyn L. Harrison
UNITED STATES

Knot Mom

Dyed, painted, hand and machine quilted; cotton, synthetic batting, dye, paint, paste resist, transparent and rayon thread; 32 by 35 in.

This piece speaks to the frustration when we are ensnared by the demands on our time.

4

5

6

4

Sue Pierce
<small>UNITED STATES</small>

Free-time Boogie

Machine pieced, appliquéd, quilted, and embroidered, hand embroidered, embellished; cotton and blend fabric, lace, CDs; 18 by 60 in. Photo: Quicksilver Photo

The quilt surface is embellished with internet-service-advertising CDs that promise hours of free time.

5

Meena Schaldenbrand
<small>UNITED STATES</small>

Innovations of the 1970s

Appliquéd, couched, machine embroidered, net overlaid; cotton, sheers, trim, CD, foil, sequins, beads, charms, lamé, beaded fringe.

This energy-efficient car is the mode of transportation back to the 1970s. Among other things, the speedometer on the dashboard is stuck at 55 mph, and the gas gauge is stuck at empty, due to the oil embargo and long lines at gas stations.

6

Jeanne Booty and Becky Davis
<small>UNITED STATES</small>

Night Mermaid

Machine appliquéd, hand embroidered and painted; commercial cotton, rayon and cotton thread; 22¼ by 33½ in. Photo: Rex-Zene Rudee

This quilt is from the series "Gone Tropical," inspired by the stories, folklore, and beauty of the Caribbean.

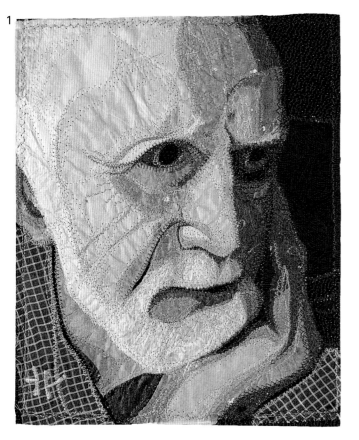

1

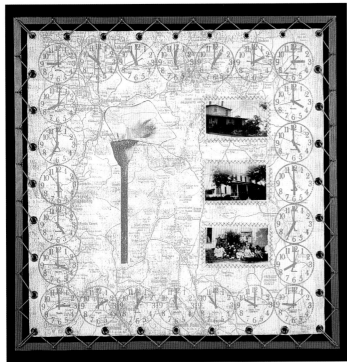

3

2

opposite page

Marna Goldstein Brauner
UNITED STATES

The Veil

Inkjet transfer, beaded; antique doll, bridal veil, beads; 17 by 6½ in. Photo: Richard Gehrke

2

Kay Campbell
UNITED STATES

The Three Fates

Screen printed, stitched, digital photo transfer; distressed cotton canvas, wood, acrylic paint, screen pigment, photographs, fiber, elastic, hardware; 22 by 22 by 4 in. Photo: Rick Gehrke

In this work, I am exploring aspects of place, origin, memory, and the passage of time. I used photographic and screen-printed images as artifacts depicting places of unknown origins.

1

Deidre Scherer
UNITED STATES

Resting on Palm

Cut, pieced, layered, machine sewn; fabric, thread, paper; 10 by 8 in. Photo: Jeff Baird

I am drawn to the pointillistic patterning of printed cloth. Fabric is the perfect vehicle with which to translate elements that are complex, non verbal, and even invisible.

3

Susan Leopold
CANADA

Rachel

Beaded, machine and hand stitched, photocopied; fabric, beads, paper; 12 by 9 in. Photo: David Saltmarche

This work was commissioned by Hadassah, New York, on the theme of Biblical women. I chose Rachel, my nine-year old daughter's name, and did it for her. Rachel signifies compassion.

1

1
Gail Ritzer
UNITED STATES

Another Star in Heaven

Hand sewn, painted, polymer transfer, collaged; water color, acrylic, fabric, and oil paint, polymer, ribbon, lace; 32 by 29 in. Photo: Henry Stindt

2
Joyce Marquess Carey
UNITED STATES

Golden Lotus

Machine and hand appliquéd, embroidered, photo transfer; silk brocade, photo transfers, cotton, polyester; 29 by 36 in.

The golden lotus was the ideal foot—only 3 inches in length. The practice of binding feet epitomizes a thousand years of suffering and subjugation of women. It was outlawed in the early 1900s.

4

3

Wendy Huhn
UNITED STATES

Girl Talk

Airbrushed, photo transfer, screen printed, machine stitched; canvas, paint,
beads, sequins, garter snaps, ribbon; 45
by 53 in. Photo: David Loveall
Photography

*I think of myself as a visual scavenger. I
borrow imagery from 18th- and 19th-
century women's magazines, books,
and pop culture. I cull, cut, and combine
imagery from my sources in an attempt
to play historical reference against mod-
ern-day culture.*

4

Agnès Bockel
FRANCE

Papier Journal

Impressed, monoprinted, pieced,
appliquéd; cotton; 45 by 50 in.

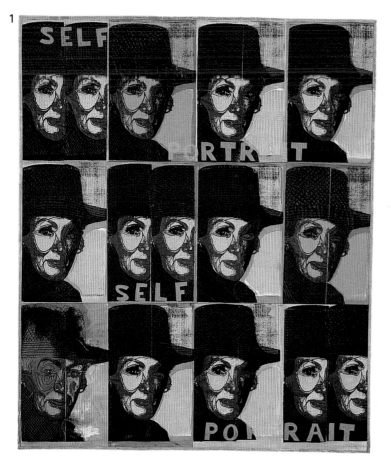

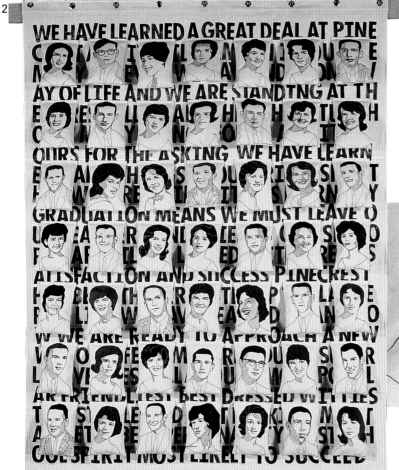

1
Jacquelyn R. Nouveau
UNITED STATES

Self Portrait

Stenciled, painted, machine stitched; linen, acrylic paint, organza; 48½ by 41½ in. Photo: Seth Tice-Lewis

My self portrait originated because I wanted to use a photo and play with an Andy Warhol look. My own photo wasn't copyrighted so I began there. When finished, I found the piece more revealing of myself then I thought it would be.

2
Faye Anderson
UNITED STATES

Dreams

Free-motion machine embroidered, fused, stamped; cotton canvas, broadcloth, hair, polyester fiberfill; 60 by 48 in. Photo: Ken Sanville

Images from my high school yearbook, circa 1967.

3
Karen Urbanek
UNITED STATES

(foot)² 1-9

Dyed, layered, manipulated, coated; silk fiber, polymer medium; 48 by 48 in. Photo: Don Tuttle Photography

I am drawn to the ordinary taken out of broader context and given precedence so that past experiences come back to me, but from an altered perspective. Familiar objects are illuminated by sensory memory and conjecture, imbued with cultural significance, providing a sense of place and personal history.

3

4

4
Clarissa Mapes
UNITED STATES

Baby Blankets

Screen printed, embroidered, sewn, burned; cotton, yarn, pigment, felt; 18 by 23 in. Photo: Jonathan Reynolds

People's habits are humorous; our tendencies are accessible fodder for satire.

5
B. J. Adams
UNITED STATES

Should Have Been

Machine embroidered, appliquéd, painted, fused; cotton, blends, felt, paint, thread; each panel 36 by 30 in. Photo: PRS Associates

Each panel represents a baseball card for a ball player from the Negro League in 1933 who never had a card. These cards/panels are of three Homestead Grays players from the Negro League that played in Washington, DC, whenever the Senators team was out of town. The panels were commissioned by Disney Entertainment for ESPN Zone in Washington, D.C.

5

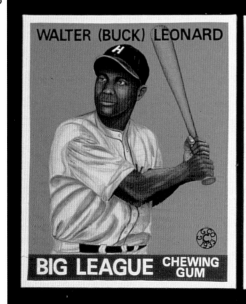
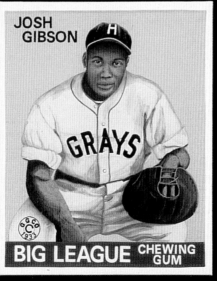
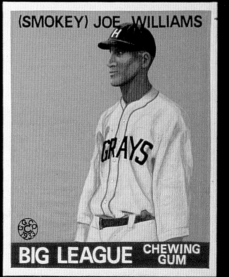

1

Peggy DeBell
UNITED STATES

Red-Shoe Magic

Computer-altered photography,
embroidered, printed, quilted,
appliquéd; cotton, embroidery
floss, beads, silk ribbon; 27¼ by
20¼ in. Photo: Tim Barnwell

*The original images in this piece
were scanned to my image-editing
software, then altered and printed
onto cotton with the use of my
inkjet machine. The holy trinity—
my computer, scanner, and
printer— brought me spiraling into
the 21st century.*

2

1

2

Beth Nash
UNITED STATES

Nude With Bird

Shibori, stenciled, airbrushed; raw
silk, foam core, fabric paint; 22 by 18
in. Photo: jerry anthony

3

Cynthia Nixon
UNITED STATES

Mirror

Painted, pieced, appliquéd, fused,
quilted; acrylic paint, cotton, canvas,
metallic fabric, plastic film, mirrors;
36 in. diameter.

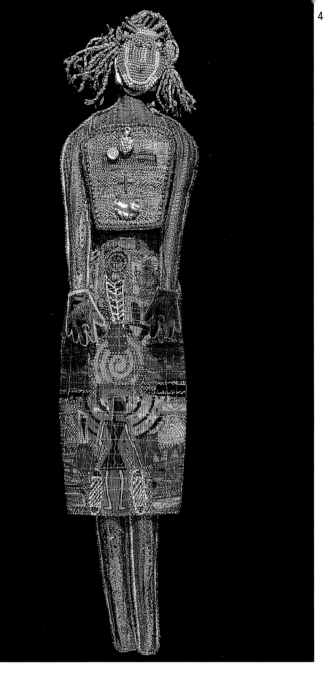

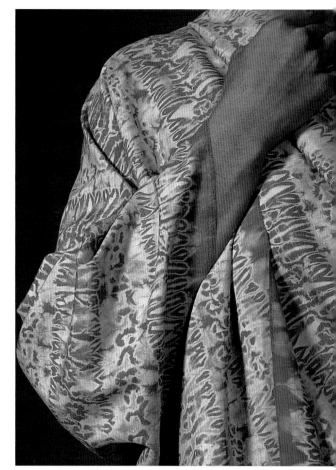

5

6

4

Lynne Sward
UNITED STATES

Personal Symbol Series #5

Machine embroidered, beaded, sewed, fused; cotton, thread, yarn, charms, transparencies, glass seed beads; 18 by 4 by 1½ in.

5

Ann Katzen
UNITED STATES

Yardage

Stitch-resist shibori; silk pongee, fiber-reactive and discharging dyes; 33 by 108 in. Photo: Eric Swanson

6

David Johnson
UNITED STATES

Persona

Photo transfer, bead embroidered, knotted; cotton/poly fabric, painted felt, beads, thread, waxed linen, painted screen; 7 by 15 by 1½ in.

1

2

1

Laura Trisiano
<small>UNITED STATES</small>

Screen

Hand painted, pieced, twisted, sewn, hammered; iron, metallic-organza silk, rayon chenille, wire, sleigh bells, beads, pearls; 76 by 54 in. Photo: Joe Tracey

Most inspiring are the ancient textiles of Asia—their pairing of simplicity with rich texture, pattern, and color. The aesthetic sensibility of our Native American peoples also stirs me deeply. Photo: Petronella Ytsma

2

Luanne Rimel
<small>UNITED STATES</small>

Portrait of a Split Second

Inkjet printed, dyed; silk, dye, graphite, ocean stone; 72 by 48 in. Photo: Lon Brauer

My work attempts to capture the ephemeral through the use of shadow images that are abstract portraits of a moment.

3

Suzanne Gernandt
<small>UNITED STATES</small>

Time and Again

Woven, printed, stamped, stitched, dyed; linen, dye, textile ink, silk and rayon embroidery thread; 18 by 12 in. Photo: Tim Barnwell

In a very real way, each composition is a meditative exercise. I am seeking that place of peace, the view of clairty that allows the viewer to establish the same within themselves. In the juxtaposition of, and interplay between, texture and pattern, intense color, and subtle nuances of shade, I seek a delicate balance.

4

Judith James
<small>UNITED STATES</small>

Ochre Patch

Screen printed, intaglio printed, discharged; cotton; 16 by 27½ in. Photo: Larry Gawel

I want my stitched landscapes to link our own experiences to those of ancient civilizations and to the natural rhythms and cycles of the universe. Referencing sky, horizon, and earth, and imagery and pattern from prehistoric stone carvings found on small objects and large orthostats, results in textile landscapes of muted color, spatial illusion, and rhythmic pattern.

5

Barbara Shapiro
<small>UNITED STATES</small>

Above All

Hand woven, ikat, shibori, discharged, painted; silk yarn, acid dye, textile paint, wood; 39 by 16 in. Photo: Sharon Risedorph

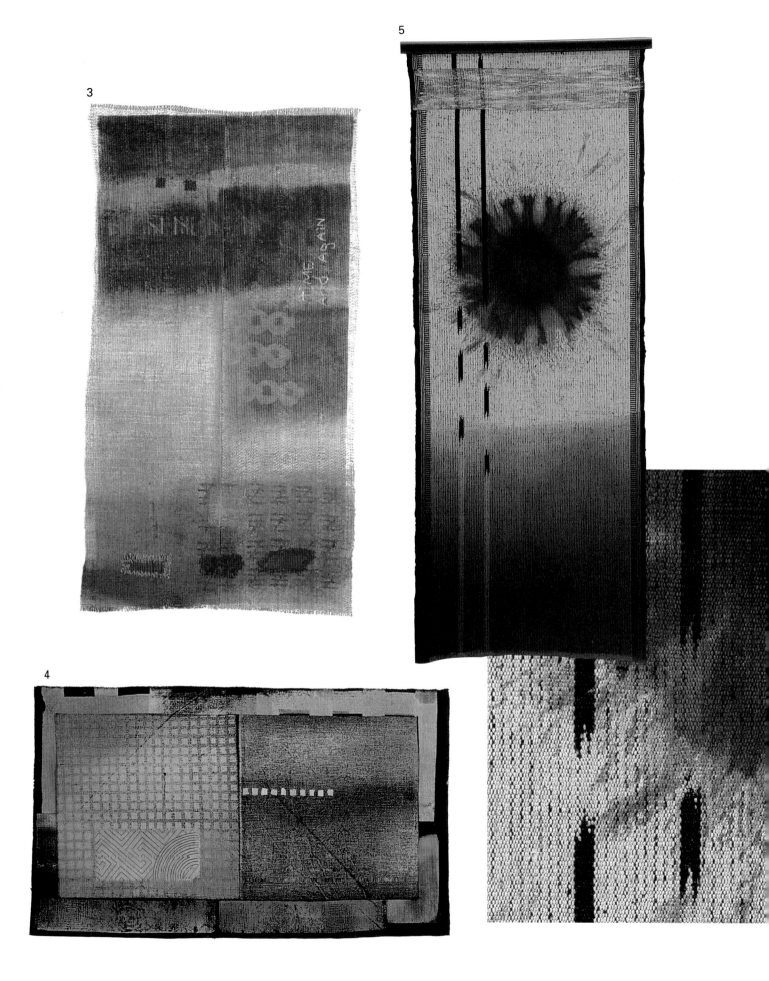

3

4

5

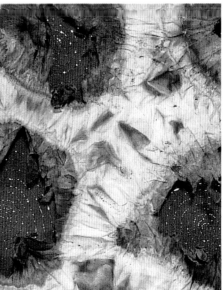

2

1
Lisa L. Kriner
United States

Ripened Thoughts

Dyed, stained, stitched; cotton canvas and print cloth, copper thread; 56 by 49 by 2 in.

I tied black walnuts into a piece of cotton broadcloth and left it in my back yard so that the walnut hulls could stain the fabric. One morning I saw a squirrel dragging my fabric in her mouth. I, of course, wanted my fabric. So we came to a compromise: if she could get at the walnuts, she could chew them out of the bundle, but the fabric had to stay. The holes she made became an important symbol of creative breakthrough in the finished art.

2
Barbara Brandel
United States

Saturday Night Fever

Hand and machine stitched, woven, threaded, twisted; buttons, wire, hardware, cloth, satin, thread, beads; 6 by 9 by 4 in. Photo: Mary Findysz Studio

Inspired by Dia de los Muertos which is celebrated in the southwest and Mexico to honor and remember the dead. They are depicted as they lived their lives.

3

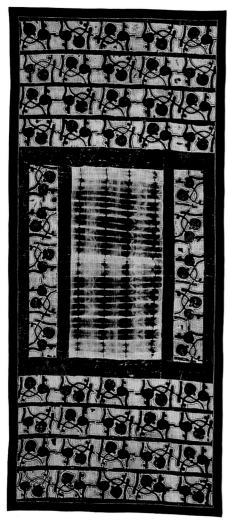

4

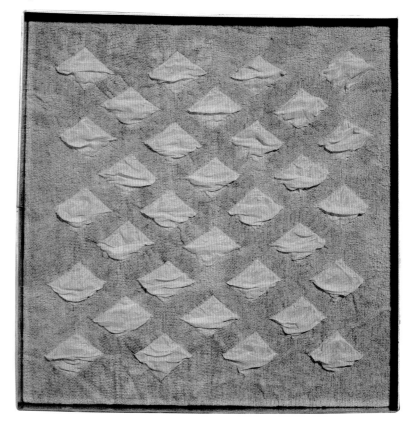

5

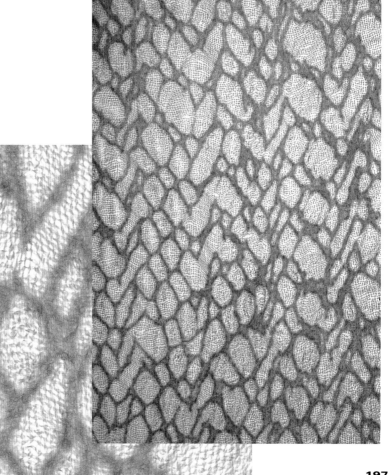

3

Susan Webb Lee
United States

Hello Darkness

Batik, discharge dyed, pleated, hand
quilted; cotton, batting, embroidery
floss; 85 by 37½ in.

4

Bitten Hansen
Denmark

Untitled B

Fused, cut, sewn; silk, cotton, linen;
11¾ by 11¾ in. Photo: Bent
Rasmussen

5

Catharine Ellis
United States

Silence and Light

Woven, shibori and felt resist, felted; merino
wool; 22 by 108 in. Photo: Kent Stewart

*Once again, my loom has given me the vocab-
ulary to explore new territory. This time, I'm
looking at the density and transparency of felted and unfelted wool cloth. The woven resist
leaves a pattern that resembles a layer of cells,
a fitting wrap for the body.*

1

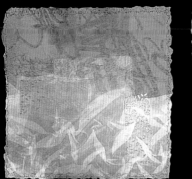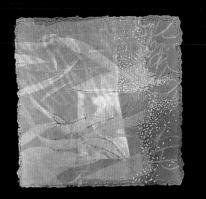

2

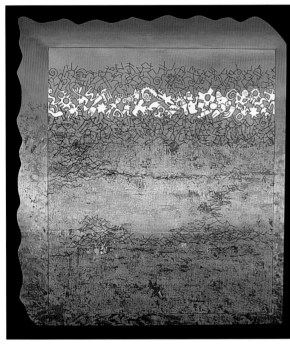

3

1
Pam Sullivan
United States

Postcards from the Shore

Heat set, transfer printed, hand embroidered, machine stitched, patinated; organza, metallic fabric, copper, cotton thread, handmade paper; 7¼ by 24 by ¾ in. Photo: Alex Pohl

I am inspired by the sea's patterns, layers, and treasures, both hidden and revealed.

2
LeAnne Beltz McDonald
United States

Six Billion

Machine stitched, appliquéd, transfers; cotton, canvas, textile paint, children's drawings, pre-Columbian images, thread; 40 by 36 in. Photo: Geof Carr

3
Judith Content
United States

Luminaria

Shibori, dyed, discharged, pieced, machine quilted; Thai silk; 59 by 68 in. Photo: Richard Johns

Even after 20 years of exploration of arashi shibori, this process of surface design never fails to fascinate and inspire me.

4
Rachel Mosler
United States

Untitled

Handstitched, waxed, stuffed; cotton, organdy, handmade paper, wax, mica, leaves, tea; 12 by 14 in.

5
Melanie Hofmann
United States

Lost at Sea

Screen printed, painted, pieced; cotton, linen, ink, dye; 38½ by 16 in. Photo: Christie Taormina

6
Teresa Paschke
United States

Clouds Know No Boundaries

Dyed, pieced, photocopied, iron-oxide transfer; cotton, nylon-gel medium, dye, graphite; 19 by 41 in. Photo: Bob Elbert

4

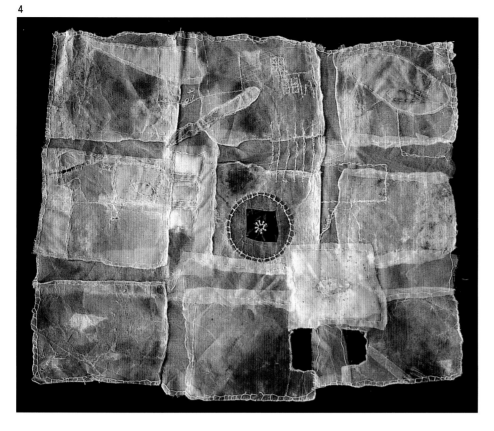

5

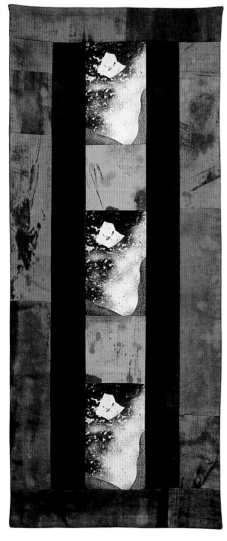

6

4

3
Kerry Phillips
UNITED STATES

Drafting the Interior: IV

Machine stitched; cotton, silk, text on paper, thread; 48 by 24 in.

I work mostly with memory—remembered, forgotten, and made up.

4
Patricia S. Roberts-Pizzuto
UNITED STATES

Map of My Memory

Drawn, sewn, dipped, collaged, embroidered; handmade paper, acrylic paint, graphite, embroidery floss, photo and tracing paper, beads, beeswax; 11½ by 15½ in.

5
Susan Brandeis
UNITED STATES

Discovered Secrets

Digitally printed, dyed, machine embroidered; cotton twill and sheeting, thread, silk organza; 50¼ by 72½ in. Photo: Mar Brandeis

For most of the past 20 years, I have been making works about nature. This grew from my love of beautiful places, the urgent need to preserve our environment, and my desire to celebrate the remaining wild places in the world. In both my choice of subjects and my choice of creative and technical processes.

1
Fran Skiles
UNITED STATES

Bird Habits III

Photo transfer, painted, sanded, sewn; paper, cotton duck, acrylic and oil paint; 45 by 31 in.

2
Wendyll Brown
UNITED STATES

Taskmaster

Hand-made paper, painted, stitched; fabric, photographs, leaves, acrylic paint, yarn, sticks; 51 by 61 in.
Photo: Colin Cooke

5

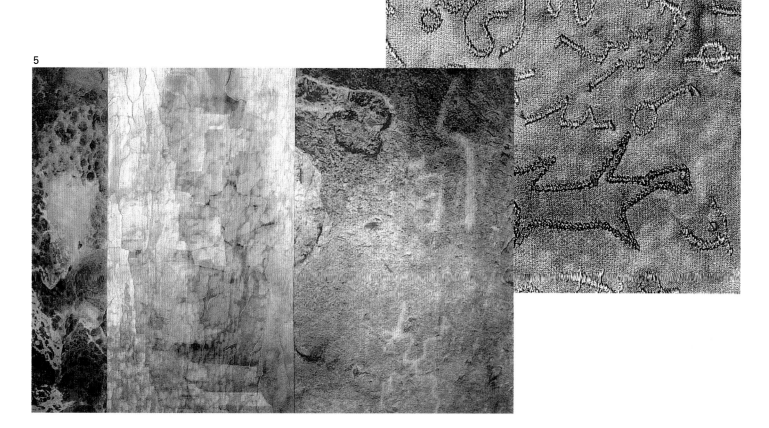

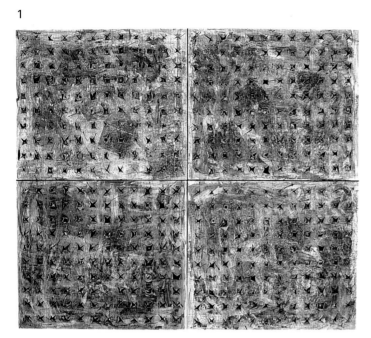

1

Marguerite Jay Gignoux
UNITED STATES

Tuesday's Sky

Collaged, dyed, stitched, screen printed, slashed; acrylic paint, canvas, hand-dyed and commercial fabrics; 84 by 100 in. Photo: Seth Tice Lewis

In response to 9/11, I created a vivid-blue urban sky and slashed it open in hundreds of places to release all the exquisite souls lost that day.

2

Lucy A. Jahns
UNITED STATES

Space/Time

Painted, machine embroidered and appliquéd; fabric, dye, thread, canvas; 28 by 47 in.

3

Els Van Baarle
NETHERLANDS

Evia

Batik, printed; silk, cotton; yardage, 43 by 157 in. Photo: Tom Kuypers

4

4

Kathleen Van Meter
UNITED STATES

Tapa Influence VII

Machine pieced and quilted, painted; window screening, wood veneer, paint; 25 by 16½ in.
Photo: John Seyfried

5

Patricia Malarcher
UNITED STATES

Diary

Machine and hand stitched, screen and transfer printed; plastic, fabric, feed sack, recycled upholstery samples; 52 by 32 in. Photo: D. James Dee

6

Diane Gilbert
UNITED STATES

Reflection Pool

Ikat dyed, warp predominant, plain weave with discontinuous weft; silk, 58 by 52 in. Photo: Alan McCoy

6

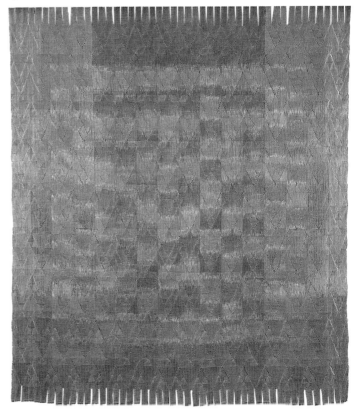

5

1

Hyangsook Park
KOREA

Readiness

Batiked, screen printed, discharged; silk, paraffin wax, ink; 21 by 24 in.

2

Mary Beth Schwartzenberger
UNITED STATES

Water Lilies

Collaged, screen printed; silk, rayon, cotton, paper; 16 by 28 in. Photo: Paul Moshay

3

Donna Durbin
UNITED STATES

Bloom

Printed, collaged, stitched; reclaimed coffee, coffee-bean bag, fabric scraps, silk, burlap, velvet, raffia; 72 by 48 in.

After a spirit quest to Bali, I returned home filled with exotic inspiration and started a new life. Hence, this piece represented a dramatic life change and transition for me.

4

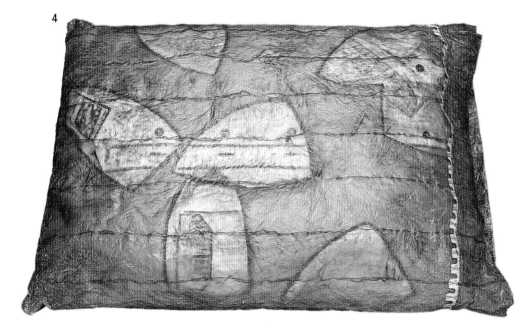

4
Emelyn Garofolo
UNITED STATES

Some Dreams are Nightmares

Dyed, constructed, assembled, scorched, drawn, couched; hog gut, man's shirt, acetate, polyester fiber-fill, non-woven interfacing, matte medium; 17 by 27 6 in.
Photo: Larry Chatterton

5
Ardyth Davis
UNITED STATES

Disc 1: Green

Dyed, pleated, manipulated, stitched, crocheted, appliquéd; Thai silk, silk cord, dye; 25 in. diameter.
Photo: Bennett Davis

6
Marie Hassett
UNITED STATES

The Offering

Paper making, stitched, collaged, drawn; handmade paper, cotton linters, abaca, silk, linen, acrylic paint, ink, beads; 15 by 18 in. Photo: Brooke Greiner

5

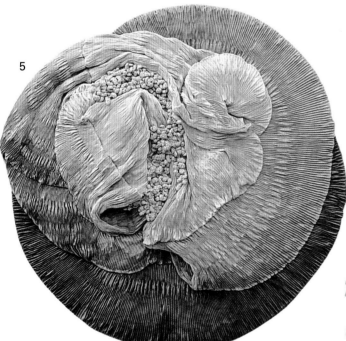

6

1

Zoe MacDonell
Australia

Documented Existence

Photocopied, hand stitched; silk, cotton, thread; 35 by 27½ in.
Photo: Ian Hobbs

2

Elina Lusis-Grinberga
Latvia

Arches of Centuries

Collaged, appliquéd, digitally printed, hand and machine stitched, hand embroidered; wool, cotton, linen; 45⅓ by 56⅓ in.

3

Hillary L. Steel
United States

Twins

Shibori, woven ikat; cotton; 21 by 16 in. Photo: Mark Gulezian

4

Jeanne Whitfield Brady
United States

Kansas: There and Back

Screen printed, vinyl transfer, potato-dextrin and chemical resist, hand and machine embroidered; silk, cotton, silk noil, organza; 15 by 40 in.
Photo: John Lucas

5

Lesley Nishigawara
United States

Holey Buchi

Dyed, burned, stitched; silk organza, natural dyes, thread; 24 by 24 in.
Photo: Mathew McFarland

Buchi (polka dots in Japanese) were created from burning many small polka dots into the cloth in all the areas except for the larger buchi areas.

3

5

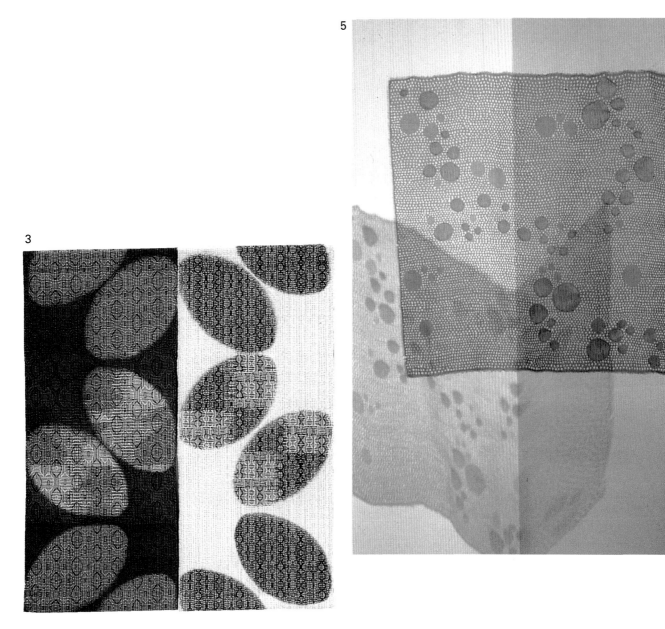

4

1

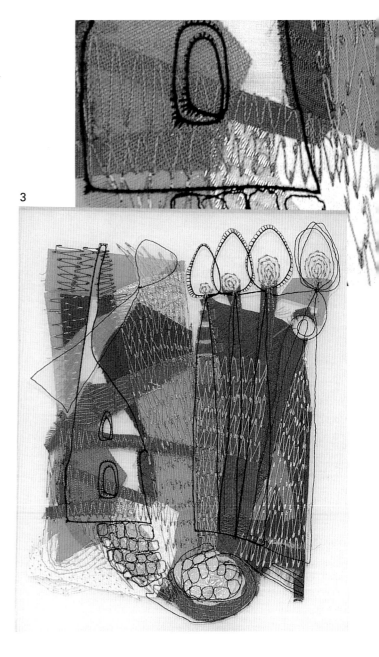

3

2

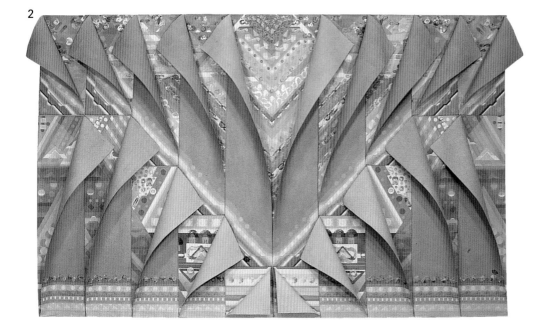

4

5

1
Kathy Alford Brady
UNITED STATES

Numinous: The Spirit of Aliveness

Hand-made paper, lino-block printed, machine stitched and quilted; kozo, abaca, cotton, twigs, paper thread, ink; 21 by 21 in. Photo: Don Rutt Photography

2
Pamela E. Becker
UNITED STATES

Carolina Vista

Pieced, sewn, painted, stamped; cotton canvas, thread, acrylic paint; 48 by 77¼ by 5 in.

Each layer contains a portion of the final image. The layers are stacked in a predetermined manner and manipulated by sewing or with ropes. When hung on a wall, the fabric layers respond to gravity, and the full image can be viewed.

3
Jenni Cadman
ENGLAND

Beacons Four

Appliquéd, machine stitched, freehand machine embroidered; cotton organdy, silk, cotton, lamé, rayon thread; 17 by 14½ in.

4
Linda Laino
UNITED STATES

Lesson

Hand felted, drawn, painted; wool felt, rice paper, watercolor, colored pencils, charcoal; 15 by 18 in. Photo: Jay Paul

5
Barbara Simon
UNITED STATES

Winter Woods

Screen printed, painted, dyed, discharged, stitched; silk, linen, cardboard, paper; 23 by 29 in. Photo: Red Elf

Inspired by the poem "Stoppng by Woods on a Snowy Evening" by Robert Frost.

1

2

3

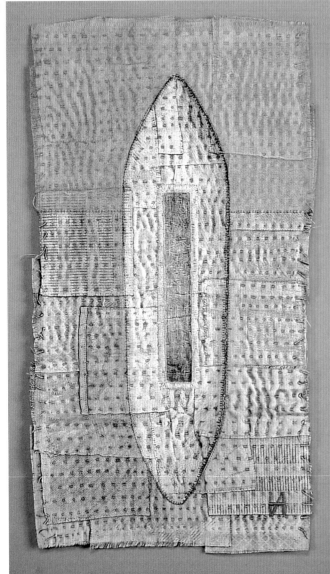

1

Heather Allen
UNITED STATES

Inquiry

Collaged, stitched, other surface design techniques; cotton, linen, silk, silver cloth, textile ink, dye; 19 by 10½ in. Photo: Tim Barnwell

2

Halina Strzechowska-Ratajska
POLAND

Romantic Landscape

Constructed, inked, sewn; corrugated cardboard, printer's ink, flax linen, thread; 94 by 49 in. Photo: Andrzej Grzelak

3

Linda McBain Cuyler
CANADA

Dancing Deer, Silver Sage

Painted, machine and hand embroidered, layered; chiffon scarf, acrylic paint, canvas, thread, fabric; 22 by 26½ in. Photo: David Cuyler

4

Jan Clark
AUSTRALIA

Cicada Toran

Hand-dyed, collaged, beaded, machine embellished; silk, glitz, iridescent beetles, glass and sandalwood beads, mirrors; 31 by 39 in.

A toran *is an embellished textile hung over doorways in northwest India. The imagery and use of reflective surfaces is very symbolic. The* toran *marks the change from the outside to the inside, secular to the sacred, or the profane to the holy. To protect the person and the space beyond the doorway, symbols and reflective surfaces are used to deflect and confuse the evil spirits who might want access to the inner space.*

5

Gwendolyn L. Kelly
UNITED STATES

"No Victim's Song"

Intaglio printed, collaged, hand embroidered, machine stitched, painted, embellished; apron, hand-printed and commercial fabric, trinkets, buttons, embroidery floss; 47½ by 30½ in. Photo: John Nation

The title of this work is from a Dianne Reeves album called "Art and Survival." Fabric collage makes me feel like an alchemist: it's magic when disparate pieces of fabric are tied together with stitching to become a story.

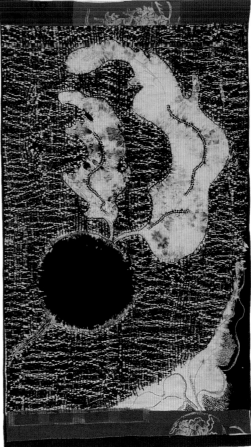

1
Carol Adleman
UNITED STATES

Heartland # 2

Appliquéd; vintage fabrics;
20 by 16 in.

2
Susan Moran
UNITED STATES

Radish

Shibori, dyed, discharged, stitched,
screen printed, collaged; silk, linen,
dye, thread; 63 by 35½ in.

3
Susan Krueger
UNITED STATES

Huis Slofje (Housewife-slave)

Discharged, painted, printed,
embroidered, quilted; cotton, ink,
paint, sequins, beads; 14 by 10¾ in.
Photo: Dave Hampshire

*Are we slaves to fashion, beautiful
to look at, but invisibly suffering?*

4

4
Carol I. LeBaron
UNITED STATES

Triptych: Collecting, Reflecting, Remembering

Pieced, clamp resisted, screen printed, acid dyed; wool, wood clamps, acid dye; each panel 96 by 30 in. Photo: Cathy Carver.

5
Beth T. Kennedy
UNITED STATES

Tonancín III

Batik, devoré, dyed, screen printed, painted, foiled, beaded, hand quilted; cotton, cotton batting, silk/rayon velvet, textile paint, foil, beads, rayon thread; 60 by 44 in. Photo: Michael Smith

This piece is named for the Aztec corn goddess whom the Spanish incorporated into the Catholic Church as Our Lady of Guadalupe. She embodies the indigenous influence in Mexico and is revered as their patron saint. Her popularity extends to Canada, and she is also celebrated as the Goddess of the Americas.

6
Sue Copeland Jones
UNITED STATES

Black Earth Grid

Discharged, painted; rayon challis, dye; 60 by 45 in.

5

6

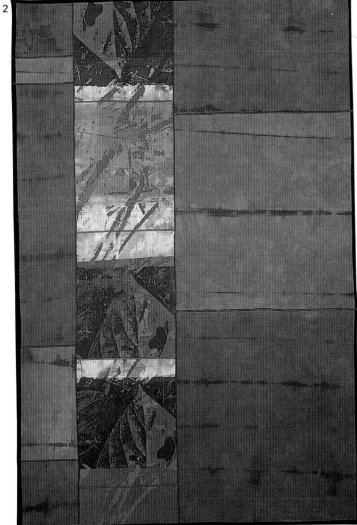

1
Sandra L. H. Woock
UNITED STATES

Potluck: Preserves

Constructed, discharged, dyed, machine quilted; cotton, cotton batting, dye; 24 by 24 in. Photo: Ken Sanville

2
Joleen Goff
UNITED STATES

Demeter's Journal

Shibori, dyed, screen printed, stitched; dye, cotton fabric; 43 by 28 in. Photo: Helios Studio

3
Robert Schwieger
UNITED STATES

The Falls at Clinton: Notes From New Jersey

Screen-printed monotype; fabric, acrylic silk-screen ink; 70 by 38½.

4
Laura Strand
UNITED STATES

Endlessly Pulling You Into the Future

Devoré, discharged, photo screen-printed, dyed; cotton damask, silk, dye; 30 by 42 by 2 in. Photo: Tony Deck

Using devoré, I am consciusly clawing through the image of a stone wall at Teotihuacán to the quilt-like surface below as a metaphor for seeing myself through the experience of Mexican indigenous culture.

5
Marla Brill
UNITED STATES

Winter's Blue

Fused, collaged, cut; linen, silk, rayon, cotton, fusible web; 30 by 30.

3

5

4

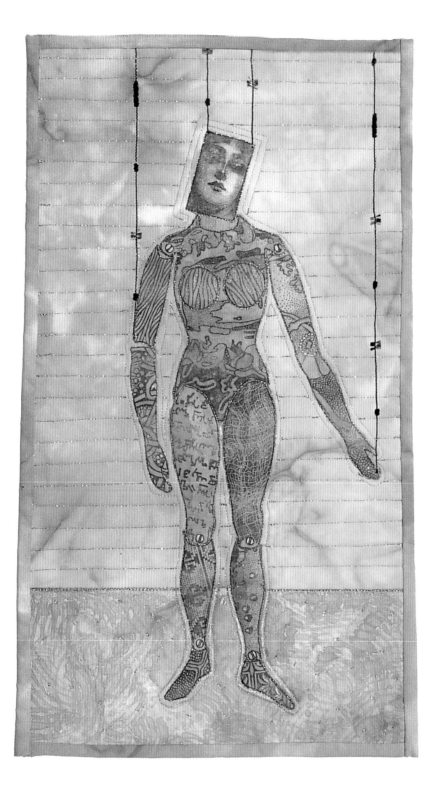

Judith Jordan
<small>UNITED STATES</small>

Controlled

Photo-carbon transfer, painted,
quilted; cotton, batting, textile paint,
thread.   17 by 9½ in.

ARTISTS' INDEX

Ann Clarke

Liz Alpert Fay

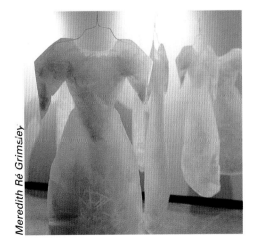

Meredith Ré Grimsley

Patricia Zobel Canaday

Susan Webb Lee

Benjia Morgenstern

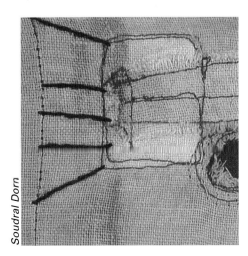

Soudral Dorn

Cecilia Voss Eager